Jean and Laurent de Brunhoff: The Legacy of Babar

Twayne's World Authors Series
Children's Literature

Ruth K. MacDonald, Editor

TWAS 824

Jean de Brunhoff
Photo by Schall

Laurent de Brunhoff
Photo by Anne de Brunhoff

Jean and Laurent de Brunhoff: The Legacy of Babar

Ann Meinzen Hildebrand

Kent State University

Twayne Publishers • New York
Maxwell Macmillan Canada • Toronto
Maxwell Macmillan International • New York   Oxford   Singapore   Sydney

PQ
2603
.R9453
269
1991

Jean and Laurent de Brunhoff: The Legacy of Babar
Anne Meinzen Hildebrand

Copyright © 1991 by Twayne Publishers

Twayne Publishers
Macmillan Publishing Company
866 Third Avenue
New York, New York 10022

Maxwell Macmillan Canada Inc.
1200 Eglinton Avenue East
Suite 200
Don Mills, Ontario M3C 3N1

10 9 8 7 6 5 4 3 2 1

The paper used in this publication meets the minimum requirements of American National Standard for Information Sciences—Permanence of Paper for Printed Library Materials, ANSI Z39.48-1984.

Printed and bound in the United States of America

Library of Congress Cataloging-in-Publication Data

Hildebrand, Ann Meinzen.
    Jean and Laurent de Brunhoff : the legacy of Babar / Ann Meinzen Hildebrand.
    p.   cm. — (Twayne's world authors series ; TWAS 824)
    Includes bibliographical references and index.
    ISBN 0-8057-8267-2
    1. Brunhoff, Jean de, 1899–1937—Characters—Babar. 2. Brunhoff, Laurent de, 1925– —Characters—Babar. 3. Children's stories, French—History and criticism. 4. Children's stories, French—Illustrations. 5. Babar (Fictitious character) 6. Elephants in literature. 7. Elephants in art. I. Title. II. Series.
PQ2603.R9453Z69   1991
843'.9120927—dc20   91-43860
                                             CIP

To my family:
Dick, Dorothy, Kay;
Bill, Jo, Chuck;
Arthur, Joanna,
and Billy

Contents

Preface

The picture book is a modern art form in which text and illustration are interwoven in a delicate tapestry. Usually intended for children, it is nevertheless sophisticated in the way it achieves meaning and emotion.[1] Artists combine the subtleties of color, design, and form in their pictures so that text is imaginatively extended, not just verified.

Illustrations have long been a part of books. The earliest manuscripts were embellished by decorative designs that added beauty and value to handwritten texts. With the advent of printing, pictures had the additional task of imparting information that confirmed some textual messages; but early methods of reproduction minimized their potential for adornment or detail. As publishing became more artful, so did pictures, and eventually the mid-Victorian English printer Edmund Evans blended beauty and utility in books attractive enough to be called "toys." Europeans, especially turn-of-the-century French artists like Boutet de Monvel and Pierre Bonnard, furthered this tradition exquisitely. Their legacy culminates in those perfect unions of word and picture, beauty and narrative—the Babar books.

Both Jean and Laurent de Brunhoff, the father and son who conceived of and preserved the unique elephant saga, are concerned primarily with creating a believably ideal environment for stories about home and family. Their imagery is, like that in most cartoon illustrations, a stylized representation of concrete, in their case usually domestic, reality. While abstraction has little place in their work, subtleties abound in the way they draw figures, design pages, and use color. Pictures and words share equally the task of creating character and setting, of developing plot and theme, of creating mood and emotion; they define, extend, and beautify one another, and only together do they make meaning.

In this study I have focused on story meanings rather than painting or writing techniques. As a responsible adult critic, I have tried to show how each de Brunhoff's distinctive skill in these arts has enhanced the stories. But I have also tried to retain the eye of childhood, which does not care why or how—only that— a story says something important, does something magical. Some grown-up readers have reduced, perhaps unintentionally, the enchantment with psychological, political, sexual, sociological, or other "adult" interpretations. Of course the Babars have serious intent—sometimes—and sometimes they have no agenda but delight. I have tried to take the serious seriously without crushing the delightful.

To that end I have relied, admittedly, on imperfect texts. Most of the de Brunhoffs' stories were composed in French; their original illustrations were watercolor paintings of great charm and artistry. The American translations I used, though more than adequately done by Merle Haas and others, could not possibly retain the exact music, rhythm, and meaning of the French words. Similarly, the various methods of reproduction, even in first editions, do not begin to capture the texture of brushwork and color in the de Brunhoff originals, as *The Art of Babar* tellingly reveals.[2] Laurent de Brunhoff himself observes, "An artist is always disappointed [about how his pictures emerge from the printing press]. . . . Sometimes I am furious, and sometimes I am just disappointed."[3] My consolation is that few readers of Babar trade books in translation have seen any but the editions I have used. It is these volumes after all, flawed though they may be, that have charmed audiences for 60 years and on which the saga's reputation rests.

I have chosen the American English editions from Random House rather than the slightly different British English editions published by Methuen because Random House has been Laurent de Brunhoff's primary publisher since the early 1960s, superseding even Librairie Hachette, which had major copyright from 1936 and still has international rights. At first mention of each book, I have given its title in the first-edition language; when that was French, as it was until the 1960s, I have also included the title and date of the first American edition. All numbering is based on first-edition pagination, which may vary widely in the plethora of reprints, adaptations, and "facsimiles." Accent markings are also bewilderingly varied. Generally, I use French spellings (Céleste, Célesteville); in quotes, however, I use first-edition markings, whatever they are.[4]

The publishing history of the Babar books is incredibly complex. They have been translated into 18 languages (and some dialects), though not all books are in all languages: Afrikaans, American, Danish, Dutch, English, Finnish, French, German, Greek, Hebrew, Hungarian, Italian, Japanese, Norwegian, Portugese, Spanish, Swedish, and Welsh. Within each country of publication, there are myriad different editions, sizes, and variations on the original stories that complicate Babar scholarships enormously but will not be addressed here. By far the most complete, probably the only, and as-yet-unpublished, chronology of international editions has been compiled by John L. Boonshaft, an American collector and scholar extraordinaire of de Brunhoff books.

"De Brunhoff books" are usually thought of as synonymous with Babar; indeed, Jean wrote only stories about the elephant-king's world. But Laurent, who continued the series after his father's death and struggled with the difficulties inherent in being a creative successor, sometimes went outside the Babars for renewal and independence. Because the non-Babar books add importantly to Laurent's distinctive Babar style, however, I have included them chronologically rather than separately, as a part of the continuum of his development.

A series as popular as the Babar books has inevitably spawned by-products over which the creators often have little control: musical compositions, films, television productions, and the attendant story and activity books; stuffed animals, china figurines, bedding, clothing, stationery, furniture, wallpaper, dishes, to name only a few. I allude to this peripheral material only occasionally. But because so much current Babariana is neither Jean's nor Laurent's work, a distinction between what Laurent calls "the commercial agenda" and the de Brunhoffs' original art will be noted.

Although I spoke often with Laurent de Brunhoff, who answered all my queries candidly, I purposely did not press for personal biographical information beyond what is already in print or is necessary to understand the stories. I did not interview any of the Paris de Brunhoffs directly, relying on published biographical data augmented by Laurent's memories, perceptions, and occasional mediations with Mme. Cécile de Brunhoff. Not having or seeking deeply privileged knowledge of the de Brunhoffs, I have, therefore, deliberately avoided glib, ill-founded historical, psychological, or sociological speculation, preferring to concentrate on the stories themselves as they reveal ideal family life.

I have included few illustrations from either man's work, believing that reductions for this format do the huge pictures a disservice. Words, even lush, leisurely ones like Nicholas Fox Weber's art criticism, cannot describe adequately the de Brunhoff oeuvre, either. The primary value of a study like this, then, is to lead readers to the books themselves, for like all art, the picture book must be personally experienced before it can be critically appreciated. The complementary magic of the de Brunhoffs' words and pictures works only when readers savor it fully, personally.

For their contributions to this study, I wish to thank the following:

Laurent de Brunhoff, *gentilhomme,* who always answered even my oddest questions with courtesy, patience, and tact; his generosity with interviews, phone calls, letters, picture permissions, and books has been invaluable.

John L. Boonshaft, whose connoisseurship, scrupulous research, and willingness to share discoveries and books have been indispensable, taught me volumes, and sharpened my zest for Babar.

Peggy Coughlan of the Library of Congress, the Interlibrary Loan Staff at Kent State University, and the Children's Room staff at Stow Public Library, without whose help I could not have located many foreign-language or out-of-print de Brunhoff editions.

Martin K. Nurmi, who photographed the pictures for reproduction.

Kent State University Research Council for funding my research travel and the Department of English at Kent State University for providing clerical support.

Ole Risom of Random House for nearly 10 years of answering my de Brunhoff questions, and Emma Dryden for her more recent help.

Multilingual friends and my son Arthur for their willingness to translate what I could not.

My daughter Joanna for her professional editorial help.

And, most important, my husband William for his insights and patience—and for being a scholar who encourages me to be one, too.

Chronologies

Jean de Brunhoff

1899 Born 9 December in Paris, the fourth child of Maurice and Marguerite de Brunhoff.

1908–1918 Educated at private Protestant schools in Paris.

1918 Inducted into French army.

1918–1930 Studies painting and works as an artist in Paris.

1924 Marries Parisienne Cécile Sabouraud, daughter of Dr. Raymond and Thérèse Sabouraud, 28 October.

1925 Son Laurent born 30 August.

1926 Son Mathieu born 28 July.

1930 Transforms Cécile's summer bedtime story about an elephant into a book for his sons.

1931 *Histoire de Babar (The Story of Babar, 1933).*

1932 *Le voyage de Babar (The Travels of Babar, 1934).*

1933 *Le roi Babar (Babar the King, 1935).*

1934 *A.B.C. de Babar (A.B.C. of Babar, 1936).* Son Thierry born 9 November.

1935 Decorates children's dining room on liner *Normandie.*

1936 *Les vacances de Zephir (Zephir's Holidays, 1937).* "Babar at Home" and "Babar and Father Christmas" serialized in London *Daily Sketch.*

1937 Dies of tuberculosis in Switzerland on 16 October.

Laurent de Brunhoff

1925 Born 30 August in Paris.

1934–1944 Educated at lycée Louis Pasteur, a public school in Neuilly.

1938 Helps finish *Babar en famille (Babar and His Children, 1938)*.

1940 Helps finish *Babar and Father Christmas* (published as *Babar et le père Noël* in 1941).

1944–1960 Studies painting and works as an artist in Paris.

1946 *Babar et ce coquin d'Arthur (Babar's Cousin: That Rascal Arthur, 1948)*.

1949 *Pique-nique chez Babar (Babar's Picnic, 1949)*.

1951 *Babar dans l'île aux oiseaux (Babar's Visit to Bird Island, 1952)*. Marries Marie-Claude Bloch.

1952 Daughter Anne born.

1954 *La fête de Célesteville (Babar's Fair, 1955)*. Son Antoine born.

1956 *Babar et le professeur Grifaton (Babar and the Professor, 1957)*, the last original-size "Big Babar" edition.

1957 *A tue-tête* (At the top of one's voice), a satire for adults.

1961 *Le château de Babar (Babar's Castle, 1962)*, published in new, smaller size.

1961–1963 Serafina books published in America.

1962 Meets Robert Bernstein and forges bond with Random House.

1963 Visits America with Marie-Claude. *Babar's French Lessons*, first of many books for Random House. *Anatole and His Donkey*.

1965 *Babar Comes to America, Bonhomme,* and *Babar's Spanish Lessons.*

1967 *Babar Loses His Crown,* first book in small, easy-reader format.

1970 *Babar's Birthday Surprise.*

1972 *Babar Visits Another Planet.*

1975 *Babar and the Wully-Wully.*

1978 *Babar's Mystery.*

1979 *The One Pig with Horns.*

1980 *Babar's Little Library.*

1981 Babar's fiftieth birthday exhibit and *Babar's Anniversary Album. Babar and the Ghost.*

1983–1984 Babar tour of nine American museums.

1983–1986 Nonnarrative "concept" books.

1984 Facsimile of *The Story of Babar,* signaling revival of original-size "Big Babar" editions.

1985 Moves from Paris to Connecticut.

1987 *Babar's Little Girl.*

1988–1991 More Isabelle stories; calendars.

1990–1991 Second Babar tour of American museums.

1990 *Isabelle's New Friend.* Marries Phyllis Rose.

Here are the babies, settled now in the garden and asleep in a big perambulator. Babar and Celeste receive the congratulations of their friends. Almost everyone brings a gift.

Poutifour, the farmer, and his wife bring fruits from their own orchard; the hens offer some eggs; the gardener some flowers. The bakers present a huge cake, and Cornelius brings three silver rattles.

The Babars present their triplets to Celesteville. From *Babar and His Children* by Jean de Brunhoff. Copyright 1938 by Random House, Inc. Copyright renewed 1966 by Random House, Inc. Reprinted by permission of Random House, Inc.

1

The World of Babar de Brunhoff

There is nothing in juvenile literature quite like the Babar stories. For 60 years, in nearly 50 picture books by two quite different men, the French elephant has been an icon for children of many nations, transcending culture, time, and class.

Reasons for Babar's enduring appeal are not hard to find. Most children love tales about animals who act and dress like exemplary people, especially exotic, powerful jungle mammals that use their trunks in authentic and imaginative ways. Youngsters also love books with big, bright, packed-full pictures that have enough delicacy and wit to be shared with parents. And they never tire of fictional friends who transform the familiar rounds of daily living into enviable adventures.

But beyond these valid enough reasons for the books' lasting popularity is their affinity with children's deeper yearnings. Centered as they are on family and home, the Babar stories offer images of love, security, and authority that comfort, reassure, and provide a safe context for vicarious independence. Every story begins at and circles back to home or wherever family is together; adventures may be faraway or risky, but home—people and place—welcomes and replenishes body and spirit. Not all real families replicate the Babars' domestic idyll, perhaps fewer than ever before; some children know home as a lonely, graceless place. For these especially, dreams are nourished by the plausible structure and detail of this elephant utopia that is a macrocosm of ideal yet possible family life.

The peculiar power of the Babars beyond other home-circling children's books is that their fictional images echo uncannily—and to an extent not found in any other series—the real world in which a father and son spent their own formative years. The de Brunhoffs poured personal credos and environments unstintingly into the stories, giving the idyll a unique authenticity that is convincing because it is true.

The milieu from which the Babars emerge covers nearly a century, from Jean's birth in 1899 to Laurent's still-creative present. In Jean's seven books, Babar's world is almost an ongoing photograph of his own world. In Laurent's 40-some books written since 1946, Babars and non-Babars alike contributing significantly if indirectly to the saga—the world is a remembered dreamscape, preserving a precious reality for children who have all too few dream images to savor in an untraditional age. To appreciate fully the artistic transformation of particular de Brunhoff reality into universal Babarian fiction, one must follow two men's lives and over 90 years of personal and cultural stability and change.

The Personal World

The world that Jean de Brunhoff lived in for at least 36 of his 37 years, and Laurent de Brunhoff for his first 12, was as close to idyllic as one comes on this earth—secure, prosperous, genteel, filled with a family love, vitality, and beauty that buffered the harsher realities of war, political upheaval, or even occasional personal uncertainty. It is the world from which Jean created his Babar stories and the one Laurent worked to sustain. That the idyll became unraveled in 1937 accounts, perhaps, for the differences in the two men's work.

Jean was born on 9 December 1899, at the hopeful dawn of a new century, to Alsatian-born Marguerite de Brunhoff and her husband Maurice, a successful Parisian publisher whose mother was of Baltic or Swedish descent and father was Austrian. Jean was the baby of the family, following some years after Cosette, Jacques, and Michel, and the darling of the well-staffed household on place Denfert-Rochereau in comfortable Montparnasse on the Left Bank.

Jean attended Protestant grammar and high school, the select L'Ecole Alsacienne behind the Luxembourg Gardens, probably imbibing the Protestant ethic, if not a religious bent, from his mother's tradition as well. Other tacit education came from the home atmosphere provided naturally by a prosperous father who valued and published about art and culture, and from the level of French society that esteemed self-control, restraint, order, *politesse*, and elegance. But the de Brunhoffs were not locked into narrow bourgeois attitudes; liberal political sympathies balanced privilege, and they were responsive to the hopeful breezes of social change that began to blow again after 1918.

Jean was just of an age to be mobilized for but miss active service in World War I; however, no Frenchman escaped its effects, and images of devastation, some of it near his mother's homeland, figure philosophically and visibly into his work. He did not follow his father and brothers into the art-and-fashion publishing business but instead chose painting as his career, studying with the fauvist Othon Friesz at the Académie de la Grand Chamière in Montparnasse and immersing himself in the rich, Louvre-centered art world of Paris. His personal refinement and restraint led him to emulate the impressionists more than the avant-garde painters that so excited art circles of the day; and his 1920s portraits and landscapes show a pleasing conservatism that is compatible with his later, great artistic achievement, the Babar books.

Never narrowly ideological, however, Jean counted as his best friend Emile (Mio) Sabouraud, a talented painter in the freer modern mode, who introduced handsome, naturally aristocratic de Brunhoff into his family. The Catholic Sabourauds were of a social class with the de Brunhoffs and welcomed Jean into what Laurent remembers as a "rather grand"[1] Right Bank house near rue Faubourg St. Honoré and its cultural riches. Dr. Sabouraud, a prominent skin specialist who practiced at home, was a generous but strict *père de famille;* he also sculpted, collected art, knew and appreciated literature—and encouraged his only daughter Cécile's career as pianist. Eventually, a natural affinity of tastes and backgrounds blossomed into love for the gracious, accomplished Cécile and Jean, and on 28 October 1924 they were married. With the financial help of both families, the young couple was able to continue their artistic careers and, while not wealthy, to live in the cultured, comfortable style they had always known.

Into this ideal setting of fond family support and gentility was born Laurent on 30 August 1925 and Mathieu on 28 July 1926. Far from disrupting the marriage idyll, the children only enriched it as Jean's young family joined older de Brunhoff and Sabouraud menages during summers and holidays in Paris and the country, delightedly mingling with grandparents, aunts, uncles, and male and female cousins whom they adored, all of whose richly varied personalities helped form the little boys' own.

Life was an orderly round of six-month summers spent swimming, playing, and exploring Grandfather Sabouraud's rambling country house at Chessy near the Marne, less than 15 miles east of Paris; four-month winters at resorts in the Swiss Alps, where Jean and Cécile taught the boys to ski in 1929; and two-month stays at the family's small flat in Paris's sixteenth arrondissement, where the boys received private elementary schooling once a week, supplemented by tutoring at home with a governess who lived and traveled with them.

Temperamentally different, quiet, self-possessed Laurent and talkative, rambunctious Mathieu were nevertheless close friends during their growing-up years. And when Cécile gave birth to another de Brunhoff "child," both little boys were there, greeting the new member eagerly. The story of how Babar was born at Chessy in the summer of 1930 is well known: how Cécile invented a tale about a little elephant, how the excited boys told Jean, and how he illustrated and expanded it into a homemade book for the family. But in the Chessy environment, everything was shared and once the picture story was seen by assorted cousins, aunts, and uncles, there was nothing but to publish it for the rest of the world.

Thus, in 1931, under the aegis of his sister Cosette's husband, Lucien Vogel, then a director of the fashion magazine *Jardin des modes*, Jean's *Histoire de Babar, le petit éléphant*, (*The Story of Babar the Little Elephant* 1933) made its debut for all the world to see. Despite an economic depression, the beautifully huge, expensive volume was such a publishing success and had given Jean so much pleasure that he quickly produced stories that developed the Babar saga further: *Le voyage de Babar* (*The Travels of Babar* 1934) in 1932, *Le roi Babar* (*Babar the King* 1935) in 1933, and *A.B.C. de Babar* (*A.B.C. of Babar* 1936) in 1934, all published by his brother-in-law's firm, a branch of the publishing giant Condé Nast. The third de Brunhoff son, Thierry, was born in November 1934. In 1936 Jean published *Les vacances de Zephir* (*Zephir's Holidays* 1937) with the French firm Hachette; the same year he did two serial stories for an English newspaper, "Babar at Home" and "Babar and Father Christmas"—altogether seven separate stories in as many years.

The Babar books were so charming and unusual that other countries clamored for translations, and English-language editions followed close on the heels of the French ones. In America, Louise Bonino Williams, who in the 1930s headed the juvenile department at Smith and Haas (eventually part of Random House), showed the large French picture book to the publisher Robert Haas. He was "so entranced" that he negotiated for American rights for the original Babar and subsequent books and for the services of his wife, Merle, who translated the expensive ($3 during the depression) books for many years.[2] Methuen published the Babars in England, where they were even more popular than in America, using British translators (though Mrs. Haas is also cited occasionally). After Jean's death international houses like Diogenes in Switzerland, Raben & Sjögren in Sweden, Masada in Israel, Aliorna in Spain, Hyouronsha in Tokyo, to name but a few of the more than 20 publishers of Babar books, also became major sources of the stories in translation.

So popular was the elephant king in his own country that Jean was commissioned to decorate the children's dining room on the French luxury liner *Normandie* with images of the beloved pachyderm. The stylized, 10-to-15-inch, light gray plywood elephants, which Laurent recalls hung in the Neuilly flat for some years, liberally decorated green walls on the luxury liner's maiden voyage in May 1935. When *Normandie*, in New York harbor for conversion, to a troop ship, burned in February 1942, the elephants apparently went up in flames; that all other artwork had been removed, however, still leaves some question about their certain fate.[3]

For the growing family, it was a prosperous, happy time in a new, larger apartment in the northwest Paris suburb of Neuilly. While summers were still spent at Chessy and winter holidays in the mountains, the older boys began regular, formal schooling in the mid-1930s at the excellent lycée Louis Pasteur in Neuilly. Laurent spent more and more time drawing, often figures of his "brother" Babar, as Mathieu honed interests that eventually led to a successful career as a pediatrician. Cécile continued her art at the piano and coordinated family routines with elegant tranquillity.

Then, as if foreshadowing events to come, Maurice de Brunhoff died in 1936; both grandmothers had died years earlier, so his passing left Jean's family with only one grandparent. Soon after, Jean, who had never been robust, learned that he had spinal tuberculosis, a disease for which the only cure at that time was fresh air and rest. And so instead of Chessy for the 1937 spring-and-summer holiday, the family stayed in Cannes and Switzerland; there they visited Jean in a TB sanatorium, where his activity was severely limited. Laurent and Mathieu had to return to Paris for school in September, saying goodbye to their father for what they sensed, Laurent remembers, was the last time. Cécile and Thierry alone were with Jean when he died in the sanatorium on 16 October 1937. The remaining de Brunhoffs and the Sabourauds joined the young family at the funeral in Paris's Père-Lachaise cemetery to bury and mourn the early death of a man they all loved.

Cécile, a widow too soon, grieved with dignity and the support of her family. But for Laurent, the eldest, Jean's death had particular reverberations, coming as it did when he was twelve and on the verge of manhood. Admiration and deep affection, if not camaraderie, had defined the son's feelings toward his father and model; Jean's place could not be taken even by caring uncles like Lucien, Mio, or Michel. In so short a time the world had spun from perpetual summer to winter.

Then hard on the heels of what must have seemed like continuous tragedy, Grandfather Sabouraud died early in 1938. The effect on Cécile and the children was traumatic; not only was a beloved, supportive father and the last *grandpère* gone, but the summer paradise, Chessy, was sold. To help the young widow, who found herself in unaccustomed financial straits, Michel de Brunhoff organized an exposition in America at which 36 of Jean's original Babar watercolors were sold. Fortunately, the two serialized stories could be completed with the combined efforts of Cécile, Laurent, and Michel, who was art director of the French *Vogue;* thus *Babar en famille* (its English title still *Babar at Home* but changed in America to *Babar and His Children*) appeared in 1938, followed by *Babar and Father Christmas* in 1940 in America and England (*Babar et le père Noël* in 1941 in France).

During these hard times, Cécile began again to give piano concerts and resumed her studies with Alfred Cortôt at L'Ecole Normale. After receiving a degree, she became professor of piano at the prestigious school, a position she held for 40 years. She had taught all her boys to play but early discerned Thierry's special talents and encouraged his study with her own teacher, Cortôt. The youngest de Brunhoff eventually became one of France's foremost pianists, a career abandoned when he joined the Benedictine order in 1974.

But no sooner was family emotional and financial equilibrium in view than the war broke out. Cécile and the children were at Mio's house near Amboise when the Germans occupied Paris in spring 1940; they spent the balance of the year in the Vendée, where the older boys even attended a lycée. But in early 1941, they returned to Neuilly and endured fuel and food shortages just like the rest of their countrymen. Both Jean and Laurent came of age during a war, but World War II struck closer to home, for though Jean's widow and sons were not personally threatened, a close friend disappeared to a concentration camp, and Michel de Brunhoff's son, a member of the Resistance, was killed by Nazis. A Frenchman maturing in the hard years from 1940 to 1945 could scarcely be blamed for looking nostalgically back to happier times and forward wishfully to peaceful ones.

Not that all was dark. Even with Chessy gone, the extended family still laughed and celebrated as well as cried and suffered together. Cécile bought a home in Velannes, near the Seine some 25 miles northwest of Paris, to which the boys often bicycled on weekends. Laurent completed his schooling at the lycée in 1944 and took a studio in Montparnasse; he began to study painting with his father's teacher, Othon Friesz, but emulated abstract artists and showed a more daring, restless style than Jean's; he was talented enough to exhibit with other promising painters at the prestigious Galerie Maeght.

However, like everyone who realistically confronts the present and future, Laurent yearned sometimes for the precious past of his childhood, the orderly reality that his father had transformed into a fictional utopia. Bringing back that world was well within his power, and in 1946, to the surprise and delight of family, friends, and Frenchmen, *Babar et ce coquin d'Arthur (Babar and That Rascal Arthur;* Methuen's title is more accurate than the American *Babar's Cousin: That Rascal Arthur,* 1948) appeared, spanning the gap since *Babar and Father Christmas* as if there had been no death, no war, no interruption.

For 15 years, Laurent continued to preserve Babar's world in six books that, except for the untypical, energetic *Babar dans l'île aux oiseaux (Babar's Visit to Bird Island* 1952) in 1951, were respectfully and determinedly faithful to Jean's conception and image of Babar. All the while Laurent also continued the uninhibited painting so essential to his "real self" at that time. In 1951 he married Marie-Claude Bloch, whom he had met through the Vogels. After daughter Anne was born in 1952, they moved to Cécile's house at Velannes where Laurent produced *La fête de Célesteville (Babar's Fair* 1955), an inventive book that was conceptually faithful to Jean's work and eventually won an award. A son, Antoine, was born in 1954, and shortly after, the family returned to Paris, taking the apartment at 49, boulevard Saint-Germaine that would be their city home for 30 years. In the 1950s Laurent juggled for the first time, and not without anxiety, three adult roles: preserver of Babar, painter-dreamer, and *père de la famille*.

Unfortunately, toward the end of the decade, Hachette, Babar's publisher since *Les vacances de Zephir* in 1936, gave Laurent the unhappy news that postwar sales of the expensive, large Babar books were lagging and an ultimatum that, if publication were to continue, they must all be reduced in size. Uncertain that he had the confidence and energy to support his family with painting alone, and fearing even more that Babar would be forgotten, Laurent felt that he had little alternative but to accede to demands, which he would later regret. The "Big Babar" editions were thus expediently "Hachetted" from approximately 10½ inches by 14½ inches and 48 or 40 pages down to 9 inches by 11 inches or less, depending on the edition, and an uncompromising 32 pages. To accomplish this, Laurent was compelled to make damaging cuts in Jean's classic stories as well as his own, abridgments that affected translations in many European countries. Hardest hit was Jean's *Babar the King,* from which the philosophically crucial dream sequence and its necessary resolution was aborted; the book ended, instead, with Babar (minus worry wrinkles) blandly in bed. Because Hachette held international rights, some editions in Finnish, Hungarian, Israeli, Italian, Norwegian, Spanish, and German suffered the same editorial disaster.

In this atmosphere of professional uncertainty, Laurent published an uncharacteristically satirical book of caricatures for adults, *A tue-tête* (At the top of one's voice 1957). Shortly after, he showed these witty line drawings to a literary agent, hoping that they could be published in the United States. That was not feasible, but Laurent did a series more suitable to the American market, the three Babar-derivative Serafina books of 1961–63 for World Publishing Co.

Meanwhile, in Paris Laurent had also met Robert Bernstein, the president-in-waiting at Random House, which had been publishing the Babars in translation since Jean's first story. Bernstein persuaded Laurent to do three new Babar books for Random House, a daring venture inasmuch as Hachette had always had first rights to de Brunhoff works. The experiment resulted in *Babar's French Lessons* (1963), *Babar's Spanish Lessons* (1965), Marie-Claude and Laurent's 1963 trip to the United States to gather material for *Babar Comes to America* (1965), and a professional relationship so congenial that Random House became Laurent's primary publisher, superseding Hachette. Even with the American firm, Laurent would be subject to publisher's economic imperatives and sometimes cajoled away from his best artistic judgments. But the connection with America was ultimately artistically, financially, and personally emancipating. Laurent was now just a little older than Jean had been at his death.

His career and Babar apparently secure, Laurent was free to create more original, nonelephant stories: *Anatole* (1963), two *Bonhomme* books (1965 and 1974), *Gregory and the Lady Turtle in the Valley of the Music Trees* (1971), and *The One Pig with Horns* (1979). He broadened the audience for Babar with easy-reader, "little-book," and small-size picture-book formats, unfortunately sometimes to the detriment of the elephant king's literary stature. And he took the Babar story beyond books. Babar Christmas cards had been advertised alongside the daily episodes of Jean's "Babar and Father Christmas," but Laurent had even greater opportunity for commercial adaptations and endorsed a variety of products in France and abroad. He authorized, but had little creative control over, several Babar enterprises of varying quality, including a French television series, a magazine, two pop-up books, and several short films.[4]

With this plethora of literary products and by-products came a personal prosperity that enabled Laurent in 1970 to buy his own summer home on the Atlantic coastal island of Ile de Re; he had given up serious (or even recreational) painting during the busy 1960s, but in his barn studio he produced Babar stories that increasingly exercised and defined his own painterly style. Nearly two decades of varied creative and commercial activity had bolstered his confidence, and the struggle between Laurent as Babar preserver and as painter-dreamer abated. The once-conflicting roles began to integrate in the fantastic *Babar Visits An-other Planet* (1972). Then in *Babar and the Wully-Wully* (1975), a completely new, Bonhomme-like character became a natural part of the elephant world. The conflict of roles was further resolved in 1980 with the delicately lyrical *Babar's Little Library,* in which the character Jean had developed in huge, bright books cele-brated the natural world as Laurent meditated on and painted it in quietly intense tiny ones. For Laurent the separation between Jean's and his stories, between Babars and non-Babars—indeed between the past and the present—was becoming artificial and unnecessary.

In 1981 Babar's fiftieth birthday was celebrated with great fan-fare. An exhibit of Jean's and Laurent's original artwork opened in Paris and later traveled to American museums; Random House published *Babar's Anniversary Album,* a compilation of three stories each, abridged from Jean's and Laurent's most successful books; following Diogenes's and Methuen's lead, the American publisher reissued *The Story of Babar,* and eventually Jean's other books, in large facsimile editions; scholarship focused on the durable series that had received relatively little serious crit-ical attention. Babar was indeed an international nursery staple, secure forever beside Peter Rabbit, Winnie-the-Pooh, Pippi Long-stocking, even Tintin; selling well in its many, varied editions; and beloved by three generations of readers.

Then, in a decidedly un-Babarian scenario (though perhaps not totally unexpected for close readers of Laurent's most recent books), Laurent de Brunhoff's marriage to Marie-Claude ended. He moved to Middletown, Connecticut, in 1985 to live in a Wes-leyan University house with professor-writer Phyllis Rose, whom he had met in Paris (and married in 1990). His startling personal "rebirth," as he calls it, emboldened him to change Babar's life too, a thing he had not felt free to do in times of less private and ar-tistic certainty. In 1987 readers were surprised but delighted with *Babar's Little Girl,* whose adventures would be part of Laurent's Babar chronicles from then on.

Such a life change entailed other career moves, not all so felic-itous. Laurent made some professional connections that seemed guided more by economic than artistic imperatives. Supporting the obviously commercial, crass use of the Babar legacy in *Babar: The Movie* (1989)[5]—thereby tacitly endorsing its myriad by-products, though he had no artistic input or control and would never have created such stories himself—Laurent helped blur the solid lines that had defined Babar in word and picture for 60 years. The danger this time was not that Babar would be forgotten but that, compared as he inevitably was to Disney's Dumbo, his dignity would be irreparably damaged by cuteness. Laurent himself acknowledged that "the real fans of Babar might be disappointed, the old fans."

Fortunately, the rest of Laurent's post-1985 activity is commendable: more little stories with Isabelle; lighthearted calendars and other artwork; affordable, uncut paperback editions (from Knopf, published first by Diogenes) of early Babars, the result of Laurent's ongoing insistence that the classic, uncut originals be accessible to all; continuation of the personal painting he had returned to after a nearly 20-year hiatus, now watercolors of restrained power; and, brightest of all, the promise—and beginnings—of a splendid new "Big Babar" in the best tradition of de Brunhoff *père et fils*.

The Larger World

The Babar stories spring from nearly a century of public as well as private contexts. At the beginning, from Jean's birth in 1899 through his creative period, the context was French, with an occasional nod to American or other un-Gallic ideas; after 1945 that encapsulated, leisurely milieu became more international, even interstellar, and reflected the fast-changing hopes and anxieties of an electronically connected world. The difference between Jean's and Laurent's generational zeitgeists naturally affects their work.

Central to the Frenchman's world in the first half of the century—and in some ways still today—was the bond and authority of *le foyer:* papa, mama, and children, their circle closely ringed by aunts, uncles, cousins, and grandparents of all generations, by blood and marriage. Roles were separate and clearly defined by tradition: papa, the head, provided for and governed the household, establishing principles and discipline; mama nurtured husband and children with affection and domestic competence, her precise duties depending on her social station; children accepted the consistent implementation of these roles and eventually achieved self-control by means of overt discipline from adults and subtle interaction with peers at play, school, or work; relatives who extended the family beyond its nuclear unit often lived in geographically close proximity to each other and assumed paren-tal roles as necessary. Joys and sorrows reverberated through these enclaves of individuals whose bonds, like the de Brunhoffs' and Sabourauds', were unquestioned.

For a family affluent enough to have property, servants, and social status, there were additional social demands: *politesse* toward those of one's own class and at least a patina of culture and education that enhanced conversational skills, gracious social behavior, and discreet personal style. Demonstrative sentimentality was thought to hinder social and professional dealings; instead, cool logic and clearheaded practicality were the likeliest paths to prosperity and that state of total well being that the French call *bonheur*. In short, discretion and restraint were the marked ideals, ostentation and vulgarity the bêtes noires of the bourgeoisie to which the de Brunhoffs, Sabourauds—and Babar—belonged.[6]

Second only to family in Frenchmen's hearts came country, and at the century's turn, France was in the temporary glow of the belle époque. After ignominious defeat by Germany in 1870 and uprisings in its North African colony Algeria, France had slowly returned to political and social stability, albeit a repressive colonial one. Some of the old national pride and prosperity, both economic and cultural, had returned to all social classes during the first decade of Jean de Brunhoff's life. This fledgling renaissance was cut short, however, by France's pyrrhic victory in World War I and the ghastly aftermath of destruction and depression. National governance fluctuated wildly in the 1920s and 1930s; the potentially stabilizing, reform-minded Front Populaire

(1936–37), which gave hope to bourgeois yet pacifist citizens like Jean de Brunhoff, was short-lived, a victim of political bickering. When the Germans came again in 1940 to occupy French soil and repress French citizens, among them Jean's widow and sons, the country was bitterly divided.

Despite its political-economic instability, the Third Republic, which endured only three years after Jean de Brunhoff, was fertile in art and culture, much of which touched the de Brunhoff (and Babar) families directly and insulated against cold political reality. In 1889 Alexandre-Gustave Eiffel built the tower that symbolizes Paris in de Brunhoff books; Maurice de Brunhoff set art-publishing precedent when he created stunning playbills for Diaghilev's 1909 Ballets russes. De Brunhoff and Sabouraud households were filled with modern books that the families discussed and nursery tales that they read to their children. Music, classical and modern, was de rigueur in both households; Francis Poulenc, one of France's avant-garde "Les Six" and an acquaintance of Cécile Sabouraud, eventually set Jean's Histoire de Babar to music.[7] The fashions of Coco Chanel and other 1920s designers were featured in Michel de Brunhoff's Vogue and worn by real bourgeois Frenchwomen (and fictional elephants). French colonial cultures, notably the North African, were celebrated in the Exposition Coloniale of 1931; like all Frenchmen, the de Brunhoffs were fascinated with its exotic animals, artifacts, and costume. Paris was a mecca for painters and sculptors, in whose company both de Brunhoffs and Sabourauds were comfortable, either as professionals or amateurs. In short, French art and culture outside the family defined the de Brunhoff/Sabouraud world and is integral to the elephant utopia as well.

At the outer limits of importance and influence in the century's early decades was the rest of the world, for most Frenchmen felt they had all they needed within their own rich hexagon: the Alps for skiing, the Riviera for sunning, Paris for haute cuisine and couture, rich farmlands for wine, colonial Algeria for sand dunes, a surfeit of great waterways—and on and on. But with the increase of transatlantic ocean travel after World War I, cultural isolation was less possible. Americans flooded Paris, and along with millionaires and artists came a unique bit of theatrical culture that caught French fancy—the minstrel show, in the form of Josephine Baker's *Revue nègre* of 1925. The exotic black performer, clad only in a tutu of bananas or feathers, became the rage among socialite Parisians during the hedonistic twenties. Though the de Brunhoffs were not of the "cabaret set," Baker's unfortunate stereotype was the talk of the town, confirming the general perception of the day—that "Negroes" were interestingly savage and often naked—and defining the way Jean de Brunhoff would ultimately think of and portray blacks.

From across the Channel in the 1920s came the Pooh books, adored and assimilated by Laurent and Mathieu and respected as much by Jean as his Babars would be by A. A. Milne. Beatrix Potter's little stories were de Brunhoff favorites, too, though neither of these English nursery classics became as widely popular in France as the Babar books would be in England. Lord Baden-Powell had launched the Boy Scout movement in England before the war, and by the 1920s its ethic of honor and camaraderie had spread to Europe; international jubilees encouraged behavior modeled on old knightly codes, the same ideals that motivated Babar and interested Jean enough to include *éclaireurs* (boy scouts) in his utopia.

When Jean wrote his last story, before he became seriously ill, the Anglo-French alliance was strong and rumblings of another world war were distant; France was optimistic and so were Jean de Brunhoff and Babar. Unfortunately, both Jean's health and world peace failed too suddenly—before the English could discover penicillin, a cure for tuberculosis, and before France and the rest of Europe could fully recover from the last war.

The fictional world of *Babar et ce coquin d'Arthur* (1946) looked the same as always. But after 1945, the real world left to Laurent de Brunhoff and his countrymen did not. France had spiritual even more than physical devastation to repair after five years of German occupation; the country anguished over internal divisions and loss of national pride. Europe and the world beyond had suffered enough to try again for international peace, committing to a United Nations that promised to be stronger than its ineffec-

tive World War I counterpart, the League of Nations. But as recovery dawned, the iron curtain fell and a worldwide cold war
chilled any spirit of reconciliation; nations again became polar-
ized; the "free" world dreaded a new kind of totalitarian autoc-
racy. Consciously or not, young, idealistic Laurent de Brunhoff
factored both the world's hopes and its anxieties into his elephant
utopia.

Progress became a race clocked by increasingly sophisticated
technology and instant communication: Who would be first in
space, on the moon, at the Olympics, with the news? Who would
be cleverest, richest, biggest, loudest? Whose state-of-the-art
weaponry would inadvertently assure a spectacular, if deadly, finish to the race? Anxiety became the unavoidable climate in which
people lived. Some of it was constructive, outward-reaching, and
led to the alleviation of inequality between races, sexes, and
classes; to a consciousness of nature's delicate balance; to humane
arts, sciences, and technologies. Other anxiety was self-centered
and destructive, leading to the erosion of family and tradition,
denial of reality through drugs, irresponsible destruction of nature, and rejection of human responsibility.

Not an exclusively post–World War II phenomenon by any
means, anxiety was nevertheless so ubiquitous during those
speeded-up decades that even stories for children, usually safe
places to dream, became as traumatic as life itself. Jean de Brunhoff's books had contained death, sorrow, and separation—but no
lasting anxiety—because his confidence in life, happiness, and
integration through family love and personal optimism made dis-
harmony only temporary. Laurent de Brunhoff's stories have no
deaths, few sorrows and separations, and exist in the same utopia; they are still far from the naturalistic stories that invaded
children's literature after 1960. But there is an undercurrent of
anxiety in his work despite, indeed perhaps because of, his determination not to replicate a real world that trusts in very little.
For Jean, anxiety was transitory; for Laurent, who acknowledged
it in his own work,[8] anxiety is inescapable. Personal psyches
aside, the home and world milieu in which each matured inevi-

tably affected how he transformed real life into the fiction of Babar.

The World of the Books

Creating a beloved, successful icon of childhood is one thing; inheriting and sustaining the legacy is another. With the best will and skill in the world, Laurent could not be, and eventually did not want to be, Jean. But Babar is resilient enough to weather differences, some more important than others, in the two men's artistic and philosophical perspectives. Ultimately, the saga is a unified, if not seamless, progression of characters, places, and adventures because both its creators trust the same imaginative idyll.

Babar's nature is, of course, fundamental to the stories. Jean formed him, if not in his own image, at least from soil he knew well. The quintessential *gentilhomme*, Babar is a courteous, responsible adult, a benevolent, honest leader, and a faithful, caring husband and father. He exceeds classic knightly restraint when he shows emotion—happiness, sorrow, worry, fear—more openly than old codes of gallantry allowed; he is more involved with his family than most upper-class fathers, personally ensuring that music, art, and literature are as integral to his children's upbringing as ethical standards and discipline. When asked about the essence of Babar, Laurent replies, "He is a good father." Indeed, Babar is the perfect *roi de la famille,* a composite of chivalric knight and Jean de Brunhoff, at the same time traditional and modern, universal and personal, drawn from ideals and reality.

He is, however, Jean's creation and persona, a fully formed legacy that Laurent did not want to alter but regarded always as "brother" rather than "self." And though Babar's name is in all Laurent's titles, Babar himself—and indeed most of Jean's familiar adults—is in the background rather than foreground of story as he was in Jean's work. Laurent focuses instead on characters that his father had been able to develop only scantly and to whom a son could relate more closely: at first it was teenage Arthur and the triplets and only gradually did he add new characters to Babar stories or create some outside of the Babars. Laurent had more freedom to capture his own ideas and times in roles that he himself could define. Unfortunately, Babar loses not only his primary role at Laurent's hand but sometimes even his authority and control; the elephant king of the sixties, seventies, and early eighties is not always a wise, calm, and resilient leader; only after Laurent's private crises were resolved did Babar regain the aplomb and gentle authority that are among his most important traits. Laurent's characters sometimes act less benignly than Jean's: children bicker and adults sometimes fail as models for behavior. Where Jean's major characters reflect his own tranquil poise, Laurent's sometimes, often unintentionally, suggest personal turmoil.

The world Babar lives in mirrors the de Brunhoffs' in rather obvious ways. Jean created Célesteville as a sort of pacifist-socialist-bourgeois paradise,[9] not unlike the idealistic Front Populaire, that ennobles both work and play, assures material bounty, supports art and science, and values family relationships. It is a place of unpolluted skies and waters, well-cultivated gardens, distinguished architecture, excellent food, and stylish clothes. Babar's world celebrates freedom with structure, self-expression with self-control. Hardships like death, war, and accident are confronted, not with despair (or prayer), but by intelligent behavior, perseverance, and optimism. The elephant utopia derives almost photographically from Jean's own roots in privileged Gallic culture, a real world secure enough to make idealism possible.

Laurent sustains that inherited world along with its major characters but acknowledges that to stay creative he "had to go outside the circle." As it was, the characters and philosophy of Babar's world did not interest him nearly so much as its environment. "I don't know that it is as a character I like him. It is the whole world that I like."[10] True to his highly visual painter's imagination, he expands the circle with new settings, augmenting Célesteville's architecture and boundaries, and combining, as Loyd Grossman shows, the real with the ideal.[11] He makes actual places like America and Normandy "elephant-friendly"; he invents fantasy worlds that make Jean's essentially domestic imagery look earthbound in a style that becomes increasingly less like Jean's.

In spite of his politically liberal attitudes, however, Jean's social perspective is, like that of bourgeois Frenchmen of his day, essentially traditional: women are wives, mothers, nurturers, the "gentle sex" whose considerable strength is mainly supportive and whose appropriate careers (if any) are limited to the arts, nursing, or teaching. Jean's females follow this model; only Zephir encounters "women" more venturesome, but only outside of Babar's world. Similarly, Jean's views of race and, to some extent, class are consistent with his own times and level of society, resulting in dated, unthinkingly insensitive treatment of blacks— who are encountered, interestingly, only outside of the elephant utopia.

Laurent inherited the females of Jean's utopia; however, he considered Céleste "too passive" and relegated her to the background along with the Old Lady, whose role was more interesting and varied. But he molds the unformed character of little Flora and, consistent with his own timely attitudes about and personal experience of strong, independent women, allows her to develop into a gently assertive female. When Isabelle is born in 1987, she has all the traditional feminine attributes but also the wide-ranging capabilities expected of modern girls. Laurent's work also reflects changing attitudes toward race. At first he adopted his father's negatively biased portrait of nonwhites. But increased sensitivity born of the times prompted him to abandon his simplistic perceptions and portray ethnic minorities in a more humane way, albeit still not including them in Babar's utopia.

Laurent characterizes Jean's drawing as "more static, serene, calm, well balanced" than his own, which is "more tense. I love movement" and change. Indeed, "where Jean elaborates, Laurent generalizes" (Weber, 109). Jean's careful, precise drawings are still pictures of moments caught in time, bodies unerringly expressive and details carefully articulated to be pored over. Laurent's are moving pictures, a form he has always admired, sometimes almost slapdash in their apparent haste and lack of minute detail but full of vitality and freedom; his line captures stance superbly too, but is more rapid than Jean's. He is daring with color, takes risks in design, and varies his style enough to satisfy his own need for movement and change. Where some of Jean's packed pictures invite long scrutiny, Laurent's urge the reader to move breezily along.

Jean's work as a whole echoes a tranquil confidence in his life and art; he is "pure, naive," more innocent and yet serious than Laurent. Jean's elephant utopia is a model of and for real life; he is not above gentle didacticism as he patiently shows how things should be in a family, a country, a world. Often witty, he uses personal imagery like de Brunhoff clothing and furniture to enrich the visual fiction, but his private humor does not exclude or condescend to his audience. Though his books justly stimulate adults' interest, Jean's clear first audience is children; he chooses details they will find and understand. In fact, Laurent says, "My father loved to show us what he was doing." He often vetted ideas with his own boys, soliciting and sometimes even heeding their child's-eye suggestions.

Laurent inherited the substance and tone of the books but inevitably shaped them to his own less paternalistic nature: "I just want to entertain and to tell a story with no message." Though some of his stories have clear—even didactic—messages, he is not as interested in guiding behavior as in creating ever-changing visual fantasy; he does not want to consider serious matters like good versus evil, as Jean did: "I would never do the Dream [in *Babar the King*]. It is a masterpiece but it is not me." Sometimes his wit is private, "to amuse myself" more than to delight young readers. Occasionally he showed his stories to his own children, but usually "I trusted my own feeling," not caring to test his work with children's opinions. His fantasy is generally more intellectual and sophisticated, less earnest than Jean's, engaging readers' minds and imaginations more than their hearts, pleasing ultimately and primarily himself.

Though Jean was by profession a painter, he took naturally to writing when he decided that his best career was making Babar books, which began, after all, with words, not pictures. His plots have dramatic point, action, and suspense; the prose style is natural and graceful, clear and direct, particularly in the early stories. Laurent captures prevailing critical opinion when he calls *The Story of Babar* "the most beautiful text . . . one of the best marvels in the world" for its elegant economy and balance. On the other hand, Laurent always defines himself as "first a painter" who enjoys and has always done writing but who sometimes finds "it hard to get a story right." His own harshest critic, he recognizes that some of his plots are thin, undramatic, and his style is often wordy. And as much as he enjoys developing picture stories, he still gets considerable satisfaction from storytelling without words, as he does in non-narrative "concept" books and calendars.

It is only fair to point out that Laurent's creative years are nearly seven times Jean's seven. If Jean's work changed in his short life, which it did, Laurent's varied even more as he matured as man and artist. Unfortunately, critics often fail to discern differences in Jean's stories, treating them as a unified touchstone of Babar excellence that Laurent never quite achieves: "Laurent de Brunhoff has none of the genius of his father," "colours are harsh," "less imaginative handling of detail," "heavier and cruder."[12] Until recently, there were no studies that evaluated Laurent's 45-year output on its own merit. And yet his best books, if not replications of Jean's beloved "bests," have their own considerable strengths that contribute to the durability and richness of Babar.

In spite of personal and stylistic differences, the de Brunhoffs have faith in the same utopia, and the benevolent philosophy of Célesteville never changes: military fanfare is fine but war is awful; all work is worthwhile if it is followed by play; troubles are transitory and best met with intelligent, optimistic perseverance. Vehicles—bicycles, cars, motorcycles, planes, balloons, rockets— often red, are ubiquitous and fascinating like the roadsters driven by urbane de Brunhoff uncles. Rivers, lakes, and oceans abound in all the Babars, and the sandy, reedy, or rural shores that surround them evoke three generations of de Brunhoff summer places; boats of all sorts, often red, travel the various waters. Clothes and demeanor are important in Célesteville, just as they were in the social environment of fashion-magazine publishers, as discreet as they are modish, in all colors and styles. The milieu is generally Gallic, with berets, thirties knapsacks, and Citroëns; *vin ordinaire,* escargots, crêpes, *baba au rhum,* and croissants; French signs, landmarks, and maps. Gardens abound: formal, vegetable, flower, hand-tended, well watered, power-mowed; birds bring news and invitations, camouflage and enhance, and appear somehow in every book. Ceremonies and celebrations, sports and pastimes, furniture and toys, art and literature, music and dance, all mirroring particular or general de Brunhoff culture, thread disarmingly through both men's books, ultimately unifying the storied world with their images. What little school there is seems pleasant, like Laurent and Mathieu's early at-home learning. There are plenty of sweets for sampling and snow for skiing. But it hardly ever rains in the elephant utopia.

In all this discussion of differences and similarities, little has been said of the humor that underlies every story, fills every picture. Just the idea of bulky gray bodies in graceful activity or colorful costume is amusingly incongruous. More overtly comic is in the way these bodies use their parts—trunks, ears, "hands," "feet," faces—simultaneously authentic, inventive, and hilarious. The books prompt tender smiles and loud guffaws with the subtlety and slapstick that Jean and Laurent do differently but equally well.

In the Babar books, the de Brunhoffs have shared and imaginatively transformed a generous segment of their real world and their dreams. But the stories are not self-conscious revelations that focus on creator more than created; they are not psychological X-rays of a father and son; and they certainly are not autobiographies of Jean and Laurent de Brunhoff. The intent of this biographical overview is not to analyze in depth the authors or their times but to shed light on moments in the books where the de Brunhoffs' lives touch and so authenticate the stories they made for themselves and children.

2

The Creation of Babar's World
Jean de Brunhoff's Stories, 1931–1933

When Jean de Brunhoff transformed his wife's story into a picture book, he was 30 years old, a mature painter, a husband and a father. He could not have known that his homemade book would become an international children's classic or that creating six more would be so artistically satisfying it would occupy the rest of his life. Even within a life so short as his, however, the stories fall into two clear groups: the early stories in which Babar's world is created and the later ones in which it is confirmed and generated.

The first flush of Jean's genius vitalizes the three stories that establish Babar's character, his physical world, and the themes both de Brunhoffs will sound. In fact, these stories are the heart of the Babars, the most interesting to thoughtful readers and students of the elephant utopia, and basic to an appreciation of the saga.

The Story of Babar the Little Elephant

In the beginning, a mother and father created a picture book story for their young sons, the eldest of whom now calls it "a masterpiece." *The Story of Babar* (*Histoire*, 1931), Jean de Brunhoff's first Babar story, is indeed an extraordinary work of art. It introduces themes, settings, and characters that will endure for three generations; its unerring economy and beauty of word and picture will be the model for two painters' best art; its story about the beginning of a family will enchant sons, daughters, and parents far beyond the summer world of Chessy.

"In the great forest a little elephant is born. His name is Babar. His mother loves him very much."[1] From these opening lines, the human child establishes identity with the tiny elephant baby in the hammock and participates in an ideal world where a caring parent "rocks him to sleep . . . while singing softly to him" (3); 31 bumptious elephant cousins and two monkeys play creatively with him in the sand; and green palm trees, solicitous birds, and sun-pink mountains protect their innocent pastimes.

But all too soon, after only three pages in fact, the idyll ends. "Babar is riding happily on his mother's back, when a wicked hunter" with an elephant gun "has killed Babar's mother!" (6, 7). The lovely ride and Babar's safe babyhood are ended; the tranquility of his life is shattered. "Babar cries" (7) and "runs away because he is afraid of the hunter" (8). The shocking suddenness of the mother's death upsets some, particularly adult, readers. Plausibly, Laurent de Brunhoff sees the event as a natural means of getting into the main story, of "making way for Babar." It is worth noting additionally that the scene was part of Cécile de Brunhoff's original nursery version perhaps because, only a year earlier, her own beloved mother, Amé, had died.

Whatever the motivation, Babar's abrupt transition from the forest womb, motherless, into a potentially lonely, alien world is not gentle. Nor is it unique, for fictional children from Snow White to Bambi and Charlotte's babies have found themselves bereaved and forced, like sad little Babar, to face the future alone, frightened, uncertain.

Fortunately, the world is not as hostile as he fears. "So many things are new to him!" (10). And, like the children who wholeheartedly mourned *The Dead Bird*[2] and then went on with life, Babar is soon distracted from his unhappiness by "[t]he broad streets! The automobiles and buses!" (*Story*, 10), and the fine clothing of gentlemen he sees near the Opera. Most happily surprising of all, he finds a new mother, "a very rich Old Lady. . . . [who] gives him her purse" (11) and thus the independence to try out this new world of the city. No longer adrift, Babar embarks on an adventure of discovery and maturation, supported by a new caring parent whose obviously bourgeois Parisian environment allows him to grow with safety and style.

Because of what Eleanor Graham calls Jean's child-directed "inventiveness,"[3] children can identify strongly with the particulars of Babar's life. Thus, the little elephant's routines of eating, sleeping, exercising, and bathing echo a real child's daily regimens in humorously incongruous ways; at the same time, they offer subtle models of how to do these activities well, for Babar, though bulky, is always mannerly, graceful, and fastidious. But he loves fun, too, and when he rides the elevator "all the way up ten times and all the way down ten times" (12), children know the thrill and understand the reprimand. With youthful relish he chooses the "grown-up" clothes that will be his trademark—"a shirt with a collar and tie, a suit of a becoming shade of green, then a handsome derby hat, and also shoes with spats" (14, 15). Then he sits with adult solemnity to have his picture taken in them. When he must learn his lessons like all children, he "is a good pupil and makes rapid progress" (22).

But soon the little elephant does things children only dream about doing. When Babar very capably drives the Old Lady's snappy red roadster through the countryside; when he leans debonairly against the mantel and regales her attentive if slightly incredulous friends with stories "all about his life in the great forest" (23);[4] and when he reminisces nostalgically about his departed childhood, "misses playing in the great forest . . . and cries when he remembers his Mother" (24), he is clearly a young man at the dawn of adulthood.

The Old Lady has always given him both structure and freedom, and so when cousins Céleste and Arthur, rambunctious living links to his forest babyhood, appear two years later, they are greeted by a self-possessed, confident Babar, a fully grown-up tutor who sets about civilizing them. First, he buys them "some fine clothes" (26) and then "takes them to a pastry shop to eat some good cakes" (27), all the while modeling correct behavior in the world of humans. The child reader's relationship with Babar has subtly changed. From now on, Babar will be an adult not a peer, a father not a brother, capable enough to guide elephants and readers into a world of grown-up adventures and achievements.

His first major adult decision is to leave his city home and return with Céleste and Arthur, whose worried mothers have come to fetch them, "to see the great forest again" (31). In a touching farewell scene, Babar lovingly embraces his dear second mother. "He promises to come back some day. He will never forget her" (32). The slim, still old lady looks sadly down on the tree-lined boulevard from her balcony and, as she watches the red car diminish in the distance, wonders, "When shall I see my little Babar again?" (33), leaving readers a little unsure that it will be soon.

Meanwhile, the old "King of the elephants had eaten a bad mushroom" (34). His death from lack of self-control is not so affecting as the senseless shooting of Babar's mother; in fact, the bilious king looks almost foolish as he crumples. And so, when the returning local hero is able to answer the elephants' call for a new ruler, the only emotion is joy. "[Babar] has just returned from the big city, he has learned so much living among men, let us crown him King" (38). Babar is honored but announces that en route Cousin Céleste and he have become engaged; if he becomes king, she will be at his side. Resoundingly the elephants accept their new royalty: "Long live Queen Céleste! Long live King Babar!!! . . . And thus it was that Babar became King" (39).

Céleste, who has grown up too, is a fitting partner for the city-educated monarch, one of his own kind who knows him well. Her gentle strength will complement rather than compete with his forceful, emotional nature. As a traditional nurturing, sensitive female, she will mirror admirably one aspect of Cécile de Brunhoff's character. Neither deferential nor passive in Jean's stories, Céleste is valued for her indispensable role in both kingdom and marriage, which are suitably launched at a spectacular coronation-wedding ceremony and dance, exceeded only by its finale. As the newlyweds face the starry night sky, obviously in love, they "are indeed very happy" (46) and "will long remember this great celebration" (47).

If the Babar books are, as I suggest, delightful universal primers on how a family should be nurtured,[5] the nurturing agents must have credibility or they will be boring didacts not to be taken seriously. In this first story, Babar is permanently legitimized by his own childhood, brief though it is, for he becomes a man the child reader has known from birth, a kind of future self who merits trust and confidence. Babar the adult is worth listening to because he has successfully accomplished his own maturity before our very eyes.

Babar "is a very good little elephant" (4), and he becomes a very good big elephant. He is an exemplary husband (and later father), friend, and king—disciplined yet spontaneous, courteous, resourceful, responsible, optimistic, considerate, imaginative, vigorous, intelligent, and above all, emotional. E. H. Gombrich applauds Jean's genius at showing Babar's variety: "With a few hooks and dots de Brunhoff could impart whatever expression he desired even to the face of an elephant."[6] Equally well, Jean draws body postures that telegraph the full range of Babar's feelings with unerring economy: rigid shock as his baby tears spill onto his dead mother; startled fear as his projectile body flees the hunter and wrinkled-skin weariness "after several days, very tired indeed" (8); sartorial pride as he sits "very elegant" before the photographic artiste (16); sybaritic delight as he sponges in a hot tub; self-satisfaction as he adroitly maneuvers the borrowed car; dejection as he weeps over remembrance of times past; gastronomic satisfaction as he savors "some good cakes," a pastime he will enjoy whenever he can; and tenderness as he embraces the Old Lady who has mothered him. His capacity for human emotional behavior is broadened in future books, where he expresses anger, worry, even despair. Never an overtly emotional man himself, Jean de Brunhoff has nevertheless not shied from endowing Babar, in both words and pictures, with feelings that make him credible to children.

Other characters who play onetime or ongoing roles establish themes and personalities important to the saga. In her short story life, Babar's natural mother creates an environment of love, music, play, and family community that will permeate the series and forecasts how Céleste and Babar will rear their own children. The rich Old Lady, a cross between tender, guiding mother and indulgent grandmother, will have influence beyond the family as musician, teacher, nurse, and partner-in-ruling; she is based on and resembles in figure Cécile de Brunhoff, whose completeness her husband needed two characters to convey! (Unfortunately, both Dorfman [37, 38] and Weber [31] wrench her out of shape.) Arthur and Céleste's mothers "are very worried" (*Story*, 29) when their children run off without telling them, anticipating other grown-ups who teach responsibility and self-control with loving discipline. Though his appearance is brief, the king-maker Cornelius, wrinkled, bespectacled, and "the oldest of all the elephants" (38), demonstrates the authority and sagacity that Babar and his family will rely on throughout his reign, until Laurent inexplicably changes him. Arthur, Céleste's spirited little brother who never gets much older, will always be there for children to smile at and empathize with.

Jean connects fantasy and reality at another level, placing his humanized elephants in a town-and-country world that is actually distorted very little. Babar quickly becomes civilized, but he is just a little elephant at the beginning, living in an elephant's natural home, part of a matriarchal elephant family that plays, shares food and waterholes, and cares for one another just as elephants do in the African wild.[7] The "great Forest" looks like any large desert oasis in colonial French North Africa, as open to ivory hunters and exploitative sportsmen then as now. Laurent recalls that his parents did not express strong antipoaching sentiments, and for himself, "it was Babar I loved, not elephants" (though he worries about the species' survival today). Thus, the shooting of Babar's mother was less propaganda than a candid depiction of likely elephant reality; the old elephant king, a natural vegetarian, also dies from a plausible cause—eating the wrong mushroom. Though highly stylized, de Brunhoff's proboscidians have authentically "lipped" trunks that serve as hands, nose, and even arms when they trumpet upward in greeting and long tusks and wrinkled skins that show age, as they do in real elephants. Like Beatrix Potter, whose books his children read before Babar was born, Jean de Brunhoff acknowledges the animal nature of his humanized characters and tries not to violate what children see when they visit the zoo. Similarly, his environments are authentic and plausible, resting, like the best fantasy, on the logic of the real world.

The dramatic shape of future stories is established here, too. This book begins with images of a home and family—*le foyer*— here a mother and child surrounded by elephant relatives. Babar is forced from that security into the world of apprehension, adventure, and discovery. At book's end, he has begun his own *foyer* and provided a perfect culmination to growing up. In future stories, the exact form of home will change: it may be a garden, the living room, a resort, the seashore; the constant will be that home is where there is family, immediate or extended. The adventure will vary in intensity: it may be an eventful honeymoon, a trip to Africa, America, or another planet; or it may be, on the calmer side, the birth of children, a fair, exploring a castle. And the happily-for-now ending may be in the nursery, around the billiard table, or going home. Whatever the specifics, however, the circular home-adventure-home pattern will organize all of the Babars; like traditional fairy tales whose shape they follow, the Babars also deliver the satisfactory ending that children expect, though happiness is realistically, not magically, achieved.

Jean de Brunhoff sets scene, tone, and character with both words and pictures, creating a balanced literary-pictorial dependence that informs the best of later Babars. Though a painter, Jean had a surprising facility with story; he transformed his wife's bedtime tale into a full-blown elephant saga, not only naming Babar[8] but eventually developing his character and adventures far beyond the expectations of this first story. His skill with words is best seen in the melodies of the original French text, where "un chapeau melon" (*Histoire*, 15) is not quite captured in the English "handsome derby hat" (15). But Merle Haas's translations are spirited and, if a little wordy, generally accurate to the concrete vocabulary, directness, and balanced pace of the original.

She is wisely faithful to de Brunhoff's present tense, common in French but not in English children's stories; "Babar *is*" lends immediacy to the action and encourages children to participate in the adventure. When this story was adapted for *Babar's Anniversary Album* (1981), it was recast into past tense, one of several unfortunate editorial decisions that seriously affected the overall quality of the volume.

Literary excellence is perhaps even exceeded by the quality of de Brunhoff's pictures. Recent facsimiles of the original, crawl-into edition, bracketed by Jean's graceful elephant-chain endpapers, reveal his skill and intent best, but even smaller, post-1960s reprints fascinate the eye. His line is simple and clean, allowing for details that might clutter a less pristine style or sure design. When Babar drives through the countryside in his natty tweed traveling suit, fully in command of his vehicle, he is clearly the center of eyes. Yet at the periphery, contributing detail without distraction, are doves, a snail, a bee, a grasshopper, a beetle, dragonflies, dogs, a goat, butterflies, cows, chickens, fish, a tugboat, a barge, fishing boats, a balloon, an airplane, a farmhouse, an orchard, a marina, a distant village, a thoughtful, pigtailed little girl, a farmer's wife, a fisherman, and a barge family! What de Brunhoff has packed into his Marne valley memory is incredible and only typical of the detail he offers in the big double pages that have no borders to limit Babar's world or the reader's imagination. The colors reproduce well: the greens, reds, and yellows are clear and uncomplicated, punctuated only occasionally by softer pink; for the quintessential starry darkness at the end, only black, gray, and silvery white are needed. Elephant-round script, which Jean did himself for this first book, is part of the artistry; when it was forfeited in the 1960s so that American children could read the text more easily, overall design suffered.

On the last page of this seminal book, picture and words unite perfectly as Babar and Céleste wave from their "gorgeous yellow" honeymoon balloon, "both eager for further adventures" (48). Then as now, readers sampled Jean de Brunhoff's sweet recipe for irresistible story and wanted more. Fortunately, even before he was sure that Babar would succeed, he gave himself the perfect transition to another adventure, a second book that many readers, including Maurice Sendak, consider his most visually stunning.

The Travels of Babar

With Babar and Céleste's honeymoon balloon freshly launched from the home pad, Arthur waves a farewell beret to the newlyweds, and Cornelius, who will rule in Babar's absence, foreshadows excitement in *The Travels of Babar* (*Voyage*, 1932), Jean's most adventurous story: "I do hope they won't have any accidents!"[9] little knowing that he will soon have reason to sigh at his own dilemmas.

In a spectacular double-spread panorama, one of Jean's best, the honeymoon couple's yellow balloon hovers over "the big blue ocean" (5) and sandy shore of an idyllic Mediterranean village. Babar's binoculars focus on a scene bursting with detail, potential individual stories, and fascinating activity. "What a beautiful journey! The air is balmy, the wind is gentle" (5). But suddenly the idyll is broken and "the balloon is . . . caught by a violent storm. Babar and Céleste tremble with fear" (6) as it flounders in a turbulent sky over unfriendly waves.

Fortunately, the balloon is blown onto an island where Babar's first concern is for Céleste's safety—"you aren't hurt, Céleste, are you?" (7)—and comfort, as he builds a fire and prepares breakfast while his bride stretches a clothesline between two amazing trees. Together they pitch the tent and enjoy "an excellent rice broth well-sweetened and cooked to perfection" (9). The reader first glimpses here the kind of marriage the Babars will have: affectionate and solicitous toward one another, cooperative in their mutually satisfactory roles, an altogether complementary team with similar tastes in food (sweet!) and pastimes.

Tranquility ends, though, when napping Céleste is tied up by "fierce and savage cannibals" (10) who inhabit the island; luckily, Babar returns from reconnoitering the island just in time, and together they "hurl themselves on the cannibals" (12), who quickly decide that elephant meat must not be very tender after all. De Brunhoff's original French reads "féroces sauvages cannibales" (Voyage, 10), with no verbal mention of their color. But he portrays the "savages" as kinky-haired, thick-lipped, spear-wielding, half-naked *black* men, justifiably offending modern readers. Even though there are "a few courageous ones who fight bravely" (13), natives—and by implication blacks in general—are shown as an ignorant, primitive lot. Jean's feather-tutued stereotype probably derives from the exotic theatrical and colonial imagery that was fascinating au courant Paris at the time[10] rather than from conscious racial prejudice. In *Babar's Anniversary Album*, Laurent edited the offensive scenes out completely, but not before he had unthinkingly perpetuated the offense in *Babar's Picnic*.

Adventure resumes calmly when a whale obligingly responds to Babar's polite request, "Could you help us to get away?" (14). They sail through smooth waters on her back until the skittish creature hungrily follows "a school of little fish" (16) and uncourteously leaves the honeymooners stranded. "'What will become of us now?' weeps poor Céleste" (17), sitting on a tiny knob in the midst of a big sea. But Babar comforts her and after some hours, the elephants on the lonely knoll attract a passing liner, which looks very much like the three-funneled *Normandie*. A lifeboat rescues them while excited passengers watch, and "a week later, the huge ship steams slowly into a big harbor" (20, 21) filled with tantalizing, double-spread prospects for adventures on shore.

But not for the Babars, for "they have lost their crowns during the storm, so no one will believe that they are actually King and Queen of the elephants" (22). With no crowns and no clothing, their identity as legitimate citizens in the world of humans has vanished. And so, instead of debarking into a tourist's paradise like the other wittily individuated passengers, Babar and Céleste are "locked up in the ship's stables," to suffer the ultimate indignity: "'They give us straw to sleep on!' cries Babar angrily. 'We are fed hay, as though we were donkeys! The door is locked!'" (23). They are only elephants!

In his first display of any but gentlemanly behavior, a furious

Babar stomps his foot, furrows his usually benign brow, and explodes, "I've had enough of this, I'm going to smash everything" (23). This time, however, Céleste is strong and controlled, wisely knowing that it is not time to cry. She calms Babar and urges patience: "Be quiet, I beg you. . . . Let's be good so [the Captain will] let us out" (23). And when the royal pair is leashed and led away by the animal trainer Fernando, Céleste again whispers, "Be patient, Babar," and is determinedly optimistic. "We will not remain long with the circus. We will get back to our native land again somehow" (25). Brunhoff is as eloquent in drawing Babar's new emotion, anger, as he was in showing the adolescent elephant's tearful nostalgia. Though the Babars never lose dignity, their demeanors are subdued, their backs turned, trunks dejectedly down, and shamed faces hidden.

But true royalty that they are, they carry bravely on and do their best in new identities that Fernando gives them along with new clothes. "Babar is . . . playing the trumpet while Céleste dances in Fernando's circus" (28, 29), and they captivate a diverse audience with their talent. In a double spread that Laurent calls the "quintessential circus masterpiece," Jean again fills the periphery with fascinating detail— an artist (himself?) who sights proportion with his thumb, enthralled families from different social classes, respectful fellow performers—but centers the picture on delicately pirouetting, tutued Céleste and impressively long-winded Babar, equal partners in survival. For at least one reader, however, this is the low point of the saga, as the noble Africans are reduced to a vaudeville act.

Though not yet free to return as monarchs of their forest arcadia, Babar and Céleste do have a homecoming of sorts when the circus visits the town in which the Old Lady, Babar's dear, remembered friend, lives. They quietly escape and make their way easily through the starry night to the house where Babar had spent his youth. "The Old Lady is overjoyed" (32), and though she cannot immediately restore their crowns, she does give them appropriate clothing, the best guest bedroom, and a civilized breakfast of coffee and croissants—no hay! If not the great forest kingdom they left, the honeymooners have returned to a home where they are known and valued. And fresh from a trip that would test any marriage, their partnership is strong.

"Babar and Céleste will not be caught again" (35) and head in the opposite direction for a change of scene before returning home. Their honeymoon travels in a balloon, on a whale, and aboard an ocean liner now continue in a red motor cab bound for the mountains where they will "enjoy the fresh air and try a little skiing" (35). And what an excursion it is, shown in what is probably the most famous Babar double spread (whose whereabouts is, unfortunately, unknown since its sale after Jean died)—a breathtaking scene of Swiss alps, chalet, hamlet, skaters, skiers, and movement that must replicate the de Brunhoffs' own ski winters. There is humor (Jean's own children pretended that the overturned skier was their inept governess), family authenticity (Babar's ski cap is like Jean's own), and historical veracity (the ski poles and body position of Babar and the Old Lady are typical of the times). The slopes' fresh chilliness have a restorative effect, and the trio is ready to return home, especially Babar, who "is anxious to show [the Old Lady] his beautiful country and the great forest where one always hears the birds singing" (38).

But the Babarian idyll is shattered once more, and when they alight from the plane, alas, "there are no more flowers, no more birds" (39), no more great forest. For while Babar and Céleste are having "accidents" (3), Cornelius and his charge Arthur, "the scamp" (26), have been embroiled in trouble of their own. In a fit of mischief, Arthur has tied a firecracker to the tail of a sleeping rhinoceros, Rataxes. At the resulting explosion, "Rataxes leaps up into the air. Arthur . . . laughs until he nearly chokes" (26). The uneasy civility between elephants and rhinos has been strained too far, and war is declared by a "furious . . . revengeful and mean" (27) Rataxes, who will be a continuing threat to all that Babar holds dear until Laurent tames him. Cornelius has reason to "feel very uneasy" and to wish, "Ah! If only Babar were here!" (27).

The war devastation that greets Babar, Céleste, and the Old Lady after their holiday is in blighted contrast to the flourishing

Alpine beauty of the previous pages. Shattered sticks that had been lushly green trees and yellow, arid earth evoke news photos of Somme battlefields during World War I. As he had when Babar and Céleste were penned like chattel in their ignominious stall, Jean shows only the trio's backs, static with dismay as if the intensity of their emotion was beyond showing. And in words of powerful restraint, he underlines their grief: "Babar and Céleste are very sad and weep as they see their ruined country" (*Travels*, 39).

But characteristically, after the moment of emotion has peaked, Babar assumes leadership again: "What is going on here?" Cornelius's explanation "is indeed bad news . . . but let's not give up" (40). Knowing well that "real war is not a joke, and many of the elephants have been wounded" (41), the monarchs carry on again, Céleste and the Old Lady as expert nurses and Babar as the elephants' leader and chief strategist. Once more grimly reminiscent of real war is the Red Cross field hospital where white-veiled nurses tend badly wounded soldiers, knowing that another "big battle will soon begin!" (41).

However, unlike malicious Rataxes, who is confident that "we will once again defeat the elephants . . . and punish that rascal Arthur" (42) by force of arms, Babar gives his soldiers fresh courage and ultimately the victory by force of mind. De Brunhoff describes the strategy: "He disguises his biggest soldiers, painting their tails bright red, and near their tails on either side he paints large, frightening eyes" (43). Eager to be forgiven, even Arthur, considerably subdued, pitches in. But it is the double-spread *picture* of elephant rumps painted like faces routing the rhinoceros horde (44, 45) that best conveys Babar's ingenuity and Jean's sense of the slapstick. "The rhinoceroses think they are monsters and, terrified, they retreat in great disorder" (45).

"Babar is a mighty fine general" (45) who deserves being carried victoriously on his soldiers' backs, the enemy vanquished and caged at his feet, to shouts of "Bravo Babar—Bravo! Victory! Victory! The war is over!" (46). War, the ultimate loss of self-control, is averted by imaginative intelligence. Babar and Céleste, magnificent in scarlet, miniver, and new crowns, honor the Old Lady for her extraordinary help by giving her gifts "and a cunning little monkey" (47).

Back home again, the monarchs "sit and chat under the palm trees" (48) with the Old Lady and her monkey who will be named Zephir. The only reminders of turmoil are broken trees in the distance; Jean de Brunhoff never overdraws an important message. But the honeymoon adventures will reverberate in one way or another throughout the Babars' reign. They have weathered adversity together in Jean's most excitingly plotted story, which touches on more serious subjects like loyalty, loss of freedom, and war—themes made palatable by his genius for transforming personal ideals and reality into nondidactic stories that provoke even children to thought. Their marriage and kingdom tested and secure, the royal couple will surely succeed at Babar's chosen work—"to try to rule my kingdom wisely . . . [and] make my subjects happy" (48).

Babar the King

No absentee monarchs, in *Babar the King* (*Roi,* 1933). Babar and Céleste begin their wise rule at home. The story's vitality, then, derives less from adventurous plot, despite some homey excitement and a stunning climax, than from richly developed theme and setting. *Babar the King* is Jean's most profound, resonant story and the philosophical center of the Babar saga.

The method of reproduction changed in this book, and for the next 30 years, de Brunhoff water color originals would be reduced to line drawings to be recolored for printing. The illustrations were not so spontaneous as in the first two books, where Jean's art was directly reproduced. But his detailed style lent itself well enough to the new technique to give this story some of his most memorable, minutely interesting double spreads.

After "a treaty of peace with the rhinoceros,"[11] home is once again a safe place for untroubled pastimes like storytelling under palm trees by the Old Lady, whose talents and importance peak in this apogee of the creation stories. But the great forest, still beautiful, is not quite complete for citybred Babar, whose adventures in the world of men have prepared him for a more complex idea of home. And so, "home" becomes further defined as Babar uses his experience of civilization to build a city, shape a kingdom, and articulate principles for informed, benevolent governance.

"This countryside is so beautiful. . . . We must build our city here . . . on the shore of the lake" (4, 5), Babar tells wise old Cornelius as they view the rush-lined water, home to flamingos, pelicans, ducks, hippos, and lush vegetation. Within moments, a dromedary caravan deposits neatly on the grass everything that Babar has brought back from his honeymoon trip—boxes of hats, records, trumpets, tools and clothes—gifts to his subjects that hint at a lifestyle that will indeed be new to them. Babar announces first to his inner circle—Céleste, the Old Lady, and Cornelius—"Now we will be able to build our city" (*King*, 7) and then tells the rest of the elephants his intentions. "This city—the city of the elephants—I would like to suggest that we name Célesteville, in honor of your Queen" (10). Fueled by the prospect of their own fittingly named heaven-on-earth, the willing subjects begin their task eagerly, under the leadership of Babar and the musical direction of the Old Lady. "All the elephants are as happy as he is. They drive nails, draw logs, pull and push, dig, fetch and carry, opening their big ears wide as they work" (9).

The small-eared Indian elephant is well known as a beast of burden. But these proud, big-eared African pachyderms are, far from servants, partners in a common goal— to build a city that they will own equally. Célesteville elephants always work hard at active, creative jobs, proud of individual contributions to the welfare of all. That Jean makes work necessary, uniformly valuable, and interesting is more to create a model of ideal but plausible society than to replicate a real political system, even one consistent with his own egalitarian sentiments. Unlike Kenneth Graham's rural utopia of leisure, *The Wind in the Willows*, de Brunhoff's is a practical place where work and play, country and city are equally desirable.

The work bears excellent fruits, and curious fish and birds are finally won over: "Come and see Célesteville, the most beautiful of all cities!" (11). Indeed spectacular, Célesteville is dominated by two symmetrically imposing buildings on a balustrade-framed hill, the Bureau of Industry and the Versailles-like Amusement Hall,[12] and two houses, one the Old Lady's and the other the Babars'; below are three tiers of smaller, identical red-shuttered, thatched huts, for "each elephant has his own house" (12, 13). The buildings all overlook the rush-fringed green lake that originally inspired Babar, now filled with elephants happily swimming, diving, playing, and boating. Order, equality, and contentment infuse the new community, which promises never to be dull because it offers a balance of stimulating activity for its residents. Only one kingly task remains for Babar to realize his dream of a civilized city: the promised gift giving.

"Babar keeps his promise. He gives a gift to each elephant and also serviceable clothes suitable for work-days and beautiful rich clothes for holidays" (14). His uniqueness as a civilized elephant had begun when he bought his green suit; Céleste and Arthur's first priority for city living had been appropriate clothing. Now Babar's subjects become urbanized and, even more important, individualized by apparel that suits perfectly each one's particular work role. (That there is an interesting mix of professionals, artisans, and manual laborers but no bankers, scientists, or clergy is perhaps a wry comment on Jean's concept of beneficial work.)

Podular sculpts in a smock and beret like the one Laurent often saw on Grandpère Sabouraud's head, and well-suited Dr. Capoulosse wears pince-nez, also part of Dr. Sabouraud's apparel. Pilophage, a military man, poses in a gold-braided dress uniform for Justinien in his painter's shirt; Olur the mechanic and Hachibombotar the street cleaner are in practical dress for their manual-labor jobs; Barbacol's tape measure and pincushion identify him as a tailor; and Coco's place in society is clearly defined by his commedia del l'arte clown dress, by which "he keeps them all laughing and gay" (24). Children wear sensible clothes to their work, which is, of course, school; the chefs' badge of office is a tall hat and white apron; firemen do their jobs in protective hats. And after the nearly disastrous honeymoon experience, Babar and Céleste are seldom without their crowns!

Indeed, hats are important to each elephant's identity and are always worn in public, often in private, and even by children. Hats confer dignity by requiring that wearers hold up their heads and walk on two legs; only elephants who have not been civilized go hatless. When Cornelius sits on the derby of status that Babar had bequeathed him at the coronation, he "was aghast, and sadly . . . [wondered,] [W]hat would he wear on the next formal occasion?" (33). Fortunately, the ever-resourceful Old Lady refurbishes this important badge of authority and Cornelius can proudly lead the big celebration of Célesteville's founding. His plumed hat is, however, no more impressive than those of the gardeners and farmers, soldiers and boy scouts, sailors and fishermen in the Workers' Parade (36, 37), whose chapeaux are a potpourri of histrionic headgear worthy of a Busby Berkeley.

That Jean de Brunhoff loved to dress in costume, perhaps natural for one of his social class and artistic inclinations, is clear from the inventiveness of his elephants' leisure wear. When they play, which is every afternoon and all day Sunday, the elephants take on new roles and "saunter about dressed magnificently" (20) in apparel that ranges from mandarins' to rajahs' outfits, from Renaissance ball gowns to Edwardian afternoon dress, from admiralty uniforms to hunting habits. At the theater, a rapt elephant audience dominated by the Royals in box seats, is resplendent with tiaras, jewels, evening gowns, and tuxedos (28, 29) in one of Jean's most famous and humorously detailed double spreads. De Brunhoff's well-dressed elephants illustrate his bourgeois conviction and experience that suitable clothes are important adjuncts to gentility but also his egalitarian insistence that everyone has a right to wear them. Undeniably, his outfits delight as they subtly teach; what readers after all, young or old, do not enjoy exploring roles by dressing up?

And what child does not also love anticipation, preparation, celebration—and dessert? In a story that centers mostly on adult activities, children empathize especially when Zephir, seduced into the kitchen to help make "cakes and dainties of all kinds" (18), falls into the vanilla cream, gets "all yellow and sticky" (19), and has to endure an expected but worth-it-all scolding and cleaning up from Céleste.

Music enriches both work and play in Célesteville. The city is built to the sounds of phonograph and trumpet; Cornelius teaches the children an ancient elephant song, perhaps not unaware of its Sanskrit origins.[13] And like Cécile de Brunhoff at her piano, the Old Lady accompanies Arthur and Zephir's Mozart duet as Céleste and Babar listen attentively on a sofa that could have belonged in Chessy. The Babars encourage musical accomplishment, as the de Brunhoffs did, and celebrate it without favoritism: "First prize for music: a tie between Arthur and Zephir" (32).

Even school is pleasant in Célesteville where the beloved teacher, the Old Lady, is "never tiresome when she teaches" (22). Her classroom is Deweyan—open, bright, interesting; individual needs and learning styles are addressed, multiplication tables are fun. Children respond ideally—by behaving well and gaining knowledge in a group environment that contrasts with Babar's pleasant but more traditional solitary tutelage in *The Story of Babar*. Schooling in the Babar books always echoes, in one way or another, though, the happy, uncompetitive mood of Laurent and Mathieu's early home tutoring.

Célesteville may be egalitarian but it is not entirely classless; de Brunhoff subtly sanctions distinctions based on upbringing, education, and interest. Babar marries a cousin, not just any elephant and certainly not a (lower-class) hippo, maintaining the social animal hierarchy suggested by Leach.[14] He and Céleste play tennis, not with the street cleaner or farmer, but with "an officer," Mr. Pilophage, and his wife; the statesman Cornelius bowls with fellow professionals Dr. Capoulosse, Fandago the scholar, and Podular the sculptor. Jean de Brunhoff was ungracious or condescending to no one, but like Babar's, his close friends were social equals. And Célesteville is a model for an ideal world based on a real one, many of whose bourgeois values Jean believed in and wanted to perpetuate.

Through his elephants, de Brunhoff implies that public virtues are but a reflection of private ones: that Babar's admirable kingdom is but a macrocosm of his household, well managed according to virtuous precepts. Jean finally articulates these guiding principles when, after the joyous anniversary parade, tragedy strikes and Babar must test the thus-far-only-implied philosophy of the saga. The Old Lady is bitten by a snake and is near death; by her hospital bed faithful "Zephir sadly remains near his mistress. She is very ill" (39). Simultaneously Cornelius, the other trusted Old One, is trapped in a house fire that he has carelessly started "and a burning beam has injured him" (41).

With images of the death-white Old Lady and bloody-browed Cornelius still in his mind, Babar goes exhausted, alone, to bed. "He shuts his eyes but cannot sleep. 'What a dreadful day! . . . Why did it have to end so badly? . . . We were all so happy and peaceful at Célesteville. We had forgotten that misfortune existed! . . . [H]ow worried I am!'" (42, 43). The euphoria following creation suddenly becomes dejection, and Babar's sleep is invaded. This time Céleste is not there to calm him.

The nightmare that follows shows just what Misfortune is: a "frightful old woman surrounded by flabby ugly beasts" (43) of fear, despair, indolence, sickness, anger, stupidity, discouragement, ignorance, cowardice, and laziness. In his dream, Babar "opens his mouth to shout: 'Ugh! Faugh! Go away quickly!' But he stops to listen to a very faint noise: Frr! Frr! Frr! as of birds" (43). And winging toward him, he sees the benevolent elephant angels of goodness, intelligence, work, patience, courage, perseverance, learning, joy, happiness, health, love and hope, armed with symbols of their virtues, "who chase Misfortune away from Celesteville and bring back Happiness" (43, 44). De Brunhoff depicts the climax of the story and, indeed, the philosophy of the saga in a memorable double spread that shows Misfortune's monsters of anxiety on the run, cowering in darkness at the bottom of the page while the more powerful angels of positive thinking soar gracefully at the top through benign pink-peach clouds.

This climactic episode has interesting if unintentional religious overtones and imagery: Babar's wise old spiritual parents are threatened by a snake in the garden and by fiery flames; Babar's solitary anxiety is akin to Kierkegaardian dread; the beasts that terrorize his dream define some of the seven deadly sins, and the angels give form to transcendentalist, mind-over-matter doctrines not unlike Mary Baker Eddy's, whose work Jean may have known. Not religious despite a Protestant education, Jean has

Babar dreams. From *Babar the King* by Jean de Brunhoff. Copyright 1935 by Random House, Inc. Copyright renewed 1963 by Random House, Inc. Used by permission of Random House, Inc.

nevertheless created for his earthly utopia a secular hell of random adversity and a heaven of self-controlled ethical behavior that I am developing in another essay.

Evil is defined and destroyed in the same picture and the same dream. It is fully vanquished when Babar greets his two old friends the next day: "Oh joy! What does he see? His two patients walking in the garden. 'We are all well again,' says Cornelius" (46). And the dream's meaning is reinforced by the Old Lady, as the extended family sits cozily in Babar's drawing room: "Do you see how in this life we must never be discouraged? . . . Let's work hard and cheerfully and we'll continue to be happy" (47). The buoyant message of Babar is no longer oblique.

The outdoor home of the opening page is now a cultivated, carpeted domicile, where Babar is so domesticated that he is smoking a pipe, like Jean de Brunhoff. And, as if to drive the central philosophy home once more, the reader is assured on the last page that "since that day, over in the elephants' country, everyone has been happy and contented" (48), as Zephir, carrying a "Long Live Happiness" flag, leads a parade of pachyderms dressed for work and play.

This scene of self-determining and therefore contented, civilized elephants satisfactorily completes the creation trilogy, synchronizing the books's themes, characters, and settings—and predicting events to come as two crowned children (Laurent and Mathieu? Flora and Pom?) and a baby in a pram (Thierry? Alexander?) march optimistically, if anachronistically, with the adults toward the future.

3

The Confirmation and Generation of Babar's World
Jean de Brunhoff's Stories, 1934–1936

After the first three stories, the creator rested. In Jean de Brunhoff's next two books, "rest" is simply a change of format and subject, as he charmingly explores Babar's world further, confirming and enriching the saga in new, vigorous ways. In his last two stories, however, though a family and a new role are generated for the elephant king, "rest" becomes a gradual loss of freshness and vitality, as Jean de Brunhoff's illness sapped his artistic and physical strength—and, indeed, his life.

A.B.C. of Babar

A.B.C. of Babar (*A.B.C.* 1934) begins the long association between the de Brunhoffs and Random House, which acquired Smith and Haas in 1936 and with it, the Babar copyright. Chronologically the midpoint of Jean's works, *A.B.C.* is a sort of bridge between his first and last three stories, echoing, augmenting, and anticipating scenes and themes that Laurent also will use.[1]

As a bridge, it has a different form from the "land mass" of the other books. *A.B.C.* is smaller; at 7 inches by 9 inches it is barely half the size of the "Big Babar" books. It is not a progressive narrative of words and pictures but a series of textless vignettes of elephant life whose packed pages often tell stories of their own.

Objects in the pictures are alphabetized according to French spellings, perhaps creating initial confusion for children who know only English. But the "List of Words to Find" on the last page provides entirely adequate translations.

These differences from mainstream Babars may account for the book's being underrated as an important part of the saga. Whatever the reason, it is often omitted from lists of Jean's works, usually ignored or misunderstood in Babar criticism, and difficult to find, by far the rarest Babar. It has been passed over for recent facsimile editions because of translation difficulties and virtually supplanted by Laurent's *Babar's A.B.C.* (1983) for the American market. Yet *A.B.C. of Babar* is one of Jean's most charming, informative books, a "breather" after his annual feats of creation.

The only text is a short introductory letter from Babar and an occasional sign, still in French; but pictures alone make eloquent meaning. Although alphabet and vocabulary reinforcement are not the book's primary focus, individual letters *are* clearly displayed in both script and print, upper- and lowercase; the glossary translations confirm details in each picture. Like many good alphabet books, this one provides discovery along with reassurance; Jean challenges and expands his young readers' vocabulary by mixing unusual, even exotic, objects and ideas with familiar ones that reinforce what they already know. Even children who cannot read get glimpses of a fascinating world that is half a century and an ocean away; those eager to try matching pictures with the French glossary reap double excitement and reward.

The first letter picture looks ahead to *Les vacances de Zephir* (1936) as six elephant children play in the branches of a leafy tree (*arbre*) as gleefully as Zephir and his brothers will do in their treetop playground. Down below are an Alsacian elephant lady in native costume (*Alsacienne*), a distinctive clown (*arlequin*), stylish egret-feathered (*aigrettes*) acrobats, and Arthur using a watering can (*arrosoir*). The scene blends present with future, exotic with familiar, and play with work in the true Babar spirit.

The *B* scene is even more domestic and, like the end of *Babar the King,* predicts royal offspring. Céleste is bathing one baby elephant (*bain, bébé*), while Babar-in-crown is offering a bottle (*bi-*

beron) to another in a cradle (*berceau breton*), a paternal task that will not usually be his. There are 14 other elephant children and various *B* objects and activities in this picture that unmistakably implies parenthood. In fact, children dominate most of *A.B.C.*'s pictures, though they are not especially evident in the first three stories.

The vintage-Babar focus of the *C* picture is a circus parade, with an eclectic audience of onlookers: a full-dress military officer (*capitaine de cuirassiers*), shoemaker (*cordonnier*), building superintendent (*concierge*), cowboy (*cow-boy!*), Céleste, and Cornélius. A pig, dog, poodle, and duck (*cochon, chien, caniche, canard*) lead the parade; Coco the clown follows, banging the bass drum (*grosse caisse*). The street is not familiar Célesteville, but because there was no city map in *Babar the King,* Jean can surprise readers on every page.

D reveals a date-palm desert oasis that is close to "the great forest" where Babar was born. Sitting under a dais, the dazzling royal visitors are greeted by citizens of this outlying area: dromedary-riding elephant legionnaires, children doing a dragon-and-devil ritual dance, and groups of caftan-clad elephant Arabs engaged in dominoes and dozing. The scene reminds readers of Babar's nonurban roots and his loyalty to the kingdom he remembers and still rules. He returns to a similar North African landscape when that rascal Arthur is stranded in an Arab village in Laurent's first book.

A parade of elephant boy scouts (*éclaireurs*) dominates the *E* scene, which shows more of Célesteville. Again, distinctively dressed spectators look on: a young Scots-elephant (*écossais*), an epauletted, starred (*étoilé*) officer, a youth on stilts (*échasses*), an elegant lady elephant with fan (*éventail*) and shawl (*écharpe*), and aproned employees of a food store (*épicerie*). As well as gaudy military costume and food, there is homage to the automobile in the form of a gas (*essence*) pump in this scene.

I and *J* take place in the Tuileries-like Célesteville gardens, with their view of the lake, formal flowerbeds, and topiary yews (*ifs*). A gardener tends hyacinths (*jacinthes*) and irises, two little elephants play Indian in costumes that anticipate *Babar's Picnic,* and a solid gentleman with binoculars (*jumelles*) reads about Japanese floods (*Inondations au Japon*) in the daily journal. The World War I nurse and soldier with a wooden leg (*jambe de bois*) are sobering reminders of war in a scene so full of peace. The logic of *K* is inconsistent but the picture is fun. Such incongruities as kangaroos in kepis and elephants in kimonos, one photographing with a Kodak (not a Canon!), coexist with cockatoos (*kakatoès*) and a "Kioto—50 KLM" road marker. But in spite of the sign, a pagoda kiosk, and a Japanese gate, the landscape is Célesteville; the Oriental robes clearly belong at the palace garden party of *Babar the King*. Laurent has been criticized for putting "alien" kangaroos in the jungle of *Babar's Picnic*, but it is Jean who first stretches geographical credulity by bringing North Africa, Japan, and Australia right to the French countryside!

L is a bedtime scene. Old Cornelius is reading a fairy tale (*Livre des mille et une nuits*) to four elephant children, one a little girl who predicts Flora of *Babar and His Children* (1938), even to the tears (*larmes*) on her cheek. Books, lilacs, toys (*lion, locomotive, Loto*), lady-fingers, and a lovely crib (*lit*) adorn the pleasant room, different in detail but identical in feeling to royal nurseries of later books.

N shows elephants backstroking, dog-paddling, diving, and flutter kicking in Lake Céleste. Close to shore, young waders are watched over by their mamas, unclothed ladies who have long, bow-tied braids (*nattes*). It is hard to say which is more absurd, the mother with two jet plaits hanging in front of her large ears or the plump, back-facing lady with the single coil that forms a continuous vertical with her tail. Both are hilariously out of keeping with established hairless elephant dignity, for in Célesteville only actors wear hair, their wigs always part of the *ensemble*.

P is the first view of Lake Céleste in rain (*pluie*), which soaks the daisies (*pâquerettes*), apple trees (*pommiers*), and paving stones (*pavés*). But even inclement weather doesn't daunt recreation-minded citizens: two paddle kayaks while another operates a houseboat (*péniche*); on shore, a landscape painter (*paysagiste*, like Jean) wields his brush (*pinceau*) as a pipe-smoking fisherman (*pêcheur*) casts his line. Heads down, an elephant family

Babar's statue watches a mountain wedding. From *The A.B.C. of Babar* by Jean de Brunhoff. Copyright 1936 by Random House, Inc. Copyright renewed 1963 by Cecile de Brunhoff. Reprinted by permission of Random House, Inc.

looks drenched despite rain gear (*pardessus, pèlerine, parasol*), apparently unaware that their enticing basket of bread (*pain*), pears (*poires*), and pâté is getting soaked!

Q reveals the busy quayside marketplace where two elephants are having a heated argument (*querelle*) outside the billiard-and-bowling hall (*Café des quilles*) as others try to restrain them. At the Salle Quinault on the opposite side of the square, totally oblivious to the violence, a queue of music lovers waits patiently for the daily chamber music concert (Quatuor de Mozart, Quintette de Schumann, Quatuor de Fauré) at matinee prices (*quatre, quinze,* or *quarante francs*). Meanwhile, an animated plum (*quetsche*) seller in a four-cornered hat (*quadrige*) hawks fruit and an old sailor solicits a handout (*faire la quête*) from a prosperous gentleman. The familiar motifs—music, work, play, food, hats—are all there, but the near-fight and indigent sailor add a puzzling tension to Célesteville's usually benign atmosphere.

R reveals more poverty in utopia: ragged clothes, rats, hard work, and not much play. An itinerant gypsy elephant family (*romanichel*) camped above the city does several jobs to support its meagre living and wagon home (*roulotte*): one woman is a chair caner (*rempailleuse*), repairing broken seats with skeins of rattan (*rotin*); a man is a skilled mender of pottery and fine china (*réparateur de faïence et porcelaine*); another is sooty from his work as a chimney sweep (*ramoneur*), and yet another intently sharpens knives on his wheel (*roue*). Two children without shoes or toys make a game of eating grapes. These gypsies seem happy enough with their industrious life; de Brunhoff's Romanies are not thieves and slackers or gigolos and dancers like so many bad Gypsy stereotypes, but it is a decidedly romantic, bourgeois conception of hard rural life.

S is a ski jump contest. The landscape is familiarly Alpine and filled with pleasant tension as all eyes in a gallery of spectators watch jumper number 76 (*sauteur soixante-seize*); they suspend eating their sandwiches and sausages (*saucisses*), while two soldiers in band hats (*shakos*) also wait to celebrate the jump (*saut*) on saxophone (*saxophone*) and tuba (*serpent, l'instrument de musique*). Watchers along the course lined with pines (*sapin*) hold their trunks expectantly for the referee to signal a good jump. The hillside Hotel Suisse and atmosphere in general echoes Babar's honeymoon, Laurent's "Little Babar" books, and de Brunhoff ski winters.

The focus of *T* is a calmer pastime, a genteel family taking tea and tart on a tulip-lined terrace overlooking a busy street. The elegantly tricorned Mama must be too warm in her fur coat (*manteau de taupe*); her children, who are musical (*tambour, trompette*), and the aproned (*tablier*) maid seem more appropriately dressed for spring temperatures. They are blissfully unaware that the street below is torn up by workers digging a trench (*tranchée*) and that a tram operator is about to bump into (*tamponnement*) a taxi. In the distance the Eiffel Tower looks down incongruously on city roofs (*toits*), a reminder that these are, after all, French elephants.

Appearing for only the fourth time (*B, D,* and *M*), in the *V* scene

Babar accompanies Céleste in a donkey-drawn cart (*voiture*), not a car, on holiday to another outlying part of his kingdom, the scenic region of vineyards (*vignobles*), orchards (*vergers*), a viaduct (*viaduc*), and a vermicelli factory (*usine de vermicelles*). The visitors are reminded that there is a speed limit (*vitesse 20 KLM*) even in this green and pleasant land (*verdure*)—which is not above tourism (*visitez le valais, vue unique*).

Three elephant children at play, two boys and a girl, satisfy *W*, *X*, and *Y* in another prophetic picture. The biggest boy has two train cars (*wagons*), the middle one a xylophone, and the little girl, a yo-yo. One cannot help thinking of Pom, Alexander, and Flora, though they would not be born until 1936, two years after *A.B.C. de Babar*, when "Babar at Home" first appeared as a newspaper serial. In *Z*, Zéphir rides a zebra at the watchful instruction of an elephant Zouave in one final nod to the affinity between Babar's extended kingdom and France's richest colony.

With intelligence and playful imagination, Jean de Brunhoff reinforces and enlarges Babar's familiar world subtly celebrating also the bounties of France—in fresh, generative images that are far more numerous than those described here. Children who do not have access to *A.B.C. of Babar,* and that is most in America today, are missing a valuable, delightful link in the Babar chain.

Zephir's Holidays

The first de Brunhoff book published by Hachette, this was another "breather," not from narrative but from the world of Babar, as the title implies. Jean began the story in 1935, when he was finishing his designs for the *Normandie*. Though he was perfectly well at the time, he did not live long enough after its publication in 1936 to fulfill the promise of this fairy tale, whose hero was Laurent and Mathieu's favorite character. Laurent did not, however, particularly like the too-passive Isabelle and chose not to perpetuate the Monkeyville settings or pursue further the "happily ever after" ending. Thus, this story stands uniquely peripheral to Jean's Babar saga, with the question, "What would Zephir and his fiancée, Isabelle, have done next?" unanswered.

"King Babar, Queen Celeste, the Old Lady, his teacher, and his beloved Arthur . . . bid [Zephir] a last fond farewell"[2] as the little monkey leaves his school-year home in Célesteville, "arrives at the station of Monkeyville and throws himself into his mother's arms" (4). He is home at last in the fanciful treetop city that has its own simian populace, government, and practical reality.

Though the reproduction does not capture Jean's subtle colors accurately, Monkeyville is a busy, pleasant community, with buildings that hang ingeniously from the branches of large, leafy trees: a restaurant complete with dining balcony, a hairdresser shop featuring stylish wigs, and architecturally creative houses that are reached by individual rope ladders (4, 5). Trains arrive at a ground-level station where the Monkey family welcomes the eldest son. "Gracious! How you've grown, my darling!" (5), says Zephir's mother, but, characteristically, the lively monkey can think only of getting home. "Let's go! Step on the gas!" (6). And

Zephir comes home to Monkeyville. From *Zephir's Holidays* by Jean de Brunhoff. Copyright 1937 by Random House, Inc.

off the parents and three siblings drive in their large red family car.

The house, "small but comfortable" (9), is a round, white, thatched building, perched high in the treetops and surrounded by a neat balcony big enough for eating and flower boxes. (Jean has secured the house with rings and nails that anchor it safely to its tree foundation, lest any young reader worry.) There is even a tree swing for Zephir's little sister and a "yard" of leafy branches in which the adventurous boys play hide-and-seek. For sweet-toothed Zephir "mother prepares a good soup of bananas and chocolate. . . . [And role-faithful] father carries up the baggage" (9).

That night, "a nightingale wakes him" (10) with a song and a message. "There's a big package for you at the station. . . . On the label is written, 'From Babar'" (11). It is usually marabous who bring important messages in de Brunhoff books; the legendary, symbolic nightingale-as-prophet suggests that this adventure may be unusual. Moonlight floods the bedroom where Zephir stands and the lake beyond, creating a mesmerizing moment of silvery stillness and sweet tension.

The next morning Zephir hurries excitedly to the railway station and finds, not the piano he had guessed, but a neat, white-and-red rowboat, which he promptly tries out, impressing the water-shy monkeys who watch from the shore. Pretty, symbolically white-clad Princess Isabelle and her father General Huc, the leader of government in Monkeyville, are admiring, too. "Oh, what a daredevil that fellow Zephir is!" (13). Appropriately, Isabelle is just the sort of beloved only child that intrepid heroes of folklore save from dragons.

Then for the first time, de Brunhoff moves from the world of humanized elephants, where disbelief is easily suspended, into the realm of conscious fantasy. Zephir, fishing silently in his new boat on the surface of the clear green water, catches a mermaid! Babar knows about watery depths that accommodate reasonable residents like whales, crocodiles, or fish. But only Zephir enters the imaginary realm of mermaids and sea witches, magical transformations and monsters—not in a dream like Babar's but in a heroic adventure.

"What's this I've caught?" Zephir exclaims, surprised at the "beautiful creature" (16) on the end of his line. Eléanore, the delicate little mermaid, implores him to leave her in the water; but like sea princesses of other magical stories, she promises, "Maybe, some day, you'll have need of me. If so, throw three pebbles into the water and repeat my name three times. No matter where I am, I'll hear you and come to you" (16, 17). The fairy tale has begun.

When Zephir returns to shore, he is greeted with disturbing news that Princess Isabelle is missing, probably kidnapped when "a green cloud . . . wrapped itself around her . . . leaving behind it a strong odor of rotting apples" (18). General Huc calls out the militia, but "in spite of all their efforts, they find no trace of her" (20). Indeed, the army, looking like French Legionnaires, is more active in Monkeyville than in Babar's city; but far from successful military dictators, as Richardson playfully suggests (183), General Huc and his soldiers are pathetically ineffectual and easily discouraged.

Mindful of Babar's philosophy, "Zephir is the only one who doesn't give up hope," and armed with "his most prized possessions: his violin and his clown costume" (22), he sets out to claim Eléanore's promise. The reliable little mermaid realizes that finding Isabelle will not be easy; nevertheless, she sets out bravely with Zephir, again like her sisters in tales of old magic, in a "gigantic sea-going shell" pulled by three fast, dolphinlike orange fish, toward "a wild-looking island . . . where my Aunt Crustadele lives" (23).

Crustadele, half mermaid and half griffin, lives in a rocky grotto and is indeed a fascinating merperson—a sibyl who uses logic based on observation rather than magic to solve this problem. The two memorable pages devoted to Crustadele's appearance and advice offer pictorial (24) and dense, but not wordy, verbal information that is as unique in Jean's work as the ancient wise one herself. Thus, "after listening to [Zephir and Isabelle] in silence" (24), she is able to tell them about the "bored . . . capricious, impatient" monster Polomoche "who smells of rotting apples . . . and has a bad habit of turning to stone those who anger him" (25). She gives Zephir an "old sack [that] will prove useful" when danger comes, and the invaluable information that "in order to succeed, you'll have to make Polomoche laugh" (25). Like many a hero of folklore, Zephir faces the task of entertaining an idle, jaded monarch as well as rescuing a princess!

But "the country looks bleak" (26) as Zephir ruefully bids farewell to Eléanore and sets off through the boulder-strewn landscape with only Crustadele's sack to disguise him (though not materially transform him, like the stock folktale "cloak of invisibility"). He remembers Polomoche's "bad habit" and is all the more distressed when, hidden by the big rocks, he "hears a gruff voice . . . [and sees] Isabelle, right in the midst of the monsters!" (28). The huge yellow Polomoche, leading the strange-looking Gogottes, threatens a weeping Isabelle: "I thought you'd be amusing . . . you do nothing but cry! . . . I'm going to change you into a rock" (29). Like many idle folk, "not savage. But . . . bored" (25), Polomoche engages in serious mischief.

At this moment, Zephir is a flawless credit to all of Babar's gentle, consistent modeling and teaching, and the essence of de Brunhoff hero—courageous, courteous, artistic, resourceful, and practical. "'Lord Polomoche, and you, Ladies and Gentlemen, permit me to salute you!' says the brave Zephir, politely, as he suddenly emerges from behind the rocks. 'I am a clown-musician by profession. Pray allow me to stop here a while, to try to entertain you'" (30).

Isabelle is delighted as Zephir begins by telling them stories about Captain Hoplala, a favorite family character that Laurent will recall in *Babar's Fair*, "and the gun made of macaroni" (31). Never terribly scary (like Maurice Sendak's Wild Things, whom they resemble—or like their own mock-deadly aura of rotting apples), the monster court takes on a look of "ease [and] a pleasant air of gaiety prevails" (31) as a pipe-smoking dog-owl, blue-spotted giraffe, green-cheeked bird-man, and other bizarre courtiers clamor for another story. But "tired of talking, Zephir dons his clown costume" (32) and, looking like Coco, nimbly executes acrobatic maneuvers in his white-face costume; he follows these antics with "waltzes and polkas, one after the other" on his violin till the monsters are "carried away by the music . . . and whirl about giddily" (34). Zephir's plan—to wear them out with pleasure—works, and "at last, tired out, they all roll over in a heap and go to sleep" (35). Zephir and Isabelle make a quiet, hasty retreat back through the boulders that were once people to the sea and Eléanore. "They are saved!" (36).

Stopping courteously to thank Crustadele, they fondly take leave of "the gentle Eléanore" (38) and return to a shoreful of family and admirers who overwhelm them with flowers and official congratulations. Even better is General Huc's promise of "my beloved daughter, Isabelle. You may marry her later on, when you become of age" (38), for a proper but open ending to this fairy tale. Thus, "Zephir goes home," first to his happy family in Monkeyville, where "they don't scold him for having gone off without telling them" (39) and eventually back to his second home, Célesteville, after "this astonishing adventure" (40). Home too is Eléanore, perched with her sisters on a rock in the sea, as the book closes with another promise: "As long as [Zephir] lives with the elephants, Eléanore . . . will watch over Isabelle" (40).

Jean de Brunhoff here affirms in a new way the importance of art, imagination, and laughter. Indeed in the Célesteville stories, the arts—music, painting, sculpture, drama, dance, and literature—are routines of daily living. And Babar could not accomplish all he does in building and ruling unless *his* clear thinking were tempered with the same imagination and humor as de Brunhoff's story making.

In this Monkeyville adventure, however, the imagination takes on new importance. Zephir must invoke the help of creatures found nowhere but in legend—a magical mermaid and her ancient aunt—before he can even get to a land of monsters and activate his real-world talents. He can free Isabelle only by entering that imaginary world, captivating it by artful strategy, and taming its savage beasts enough to go home again to reality. Thus Zephir solves a problem of the real world—finding a lost child— by applying his Célesteville-honed arts in an imaginary one. In *Babar the King,* the angelic heralds of happiness—hope, love, intelligence, work, patience, courage, learning, goodness, perseverance, and joy—chased the monsters of misfortune. But Zephir needed yet another weapon to resist Polomoche and the Gogottes. Here Jean de Brunhoff suggests that moral virtues must be informed by the constructive fancy of imagination, as he expounds consciously and delightedly on the meaning of "play . . . and dream" (*King*, 26).

Babar and His Children

Jean de Brunhoff was "not quite well" when he wrote this, his most intimate and autobiographical narrative, in 1936. Though Bettina Hurlimann suggests that his illness lasted for most of his career in writing picture books,[3] Laurent says that "her description of my father's illness is pure fantasy. . . . He was really ill only the last year of his life and it never crossed his mind that he might die young when writing and illustrating his Babar books."

The story was published first as a longer, midyear, black-and-white serial in London's *Daily Sketch* and titled "Babar at Home." Its posthumous appearance in book form came only after considerable rewriting by Cécile and some coloring by Laurent, both under the artistic direction of Jean's brother Michel. Its style is not as verbally direct as the first stories, tending sometimes toward wordiness; some double spreads lack Jean's exquisite detail, drawn as they were to newspaper scale; and the plot is rambling, as if to fit short, daily episodes. Yet this is one of Jean's best-loved books: Babar is sobered and matured by fatherhood—and his family suddenly numbers five, like the de Brunhoffs'.

Babar is at home in the cozy living room where he tells Cornelius, "Old Friend . . . Celeste, my wife, has just told me that she is expecting a baby."[4] He receives his senior advisor's courteous congratulations and commissions him to announce the good news to all the residents of Célesteville. Resplendent in "full-dress uniform" (4) and imposing new admiral's hat, Cornelius reads Babar's typically solicitous proclamation to his "Dear and Loyal Subjects / When you hear a salute fired from a cannon, do not be alarmed. It will not mean that another war has begun, but simply that a little baby has been born to your King and Queen . . . In this way you will all learn the glorious tidings at the same time. / Long live the future Mother, your Queen Céleste!" (6).

Babar, who has narrowly escaped death and servitude, won a war, and built a city, is nevertheless anxious in this new situation, imagining and "thinking [only] of his wife and the little baby soon to be born" (7) as he tries to read, write, and garden. Céleste, ever attuned to her mate's emotions, "urges him to go for a ride on his bicycle, to take his mind off the big event" (8). He finds a peaceful knoll overlooking the lake where he puffs his pipe and contentedly awaits the birth.

Then "Boom!"—not once but three times, as the "Artillery Captain . . . carries out the orders he has just received" (9), making everyone, especially Babar, puzzled at the three shots. "He immediately mounts his bicycle" and, a picture of downhill-biking intensity, "rides home as fast as he can pedal" (9), "dashes headlong up the stairs, joyfully rushes into Celeste's bedchamber and embraces his wife tenderly" (10). Conveyed in these economical, action-packed phrases is the momentum of a new father's excitement. Jean, after all, was not far from his own memory of Thierry's birth, and as Laurent says, "to see the baby in his first years certainly gave Jean the idea of giving children to Babar." Céleste "smiles and proudly shows him three little baby elephants . . . a surprise to find . . . when you only expected one!" (11). The experienced Old Lady and a nurse are there, too, to help hold and later provide a makeshift bed to keep the unexpected royal babies sheltered and warm. The triplets' "off-camera" delivery in a homelike setting (perhaps a private clinic like the one in which the de Brunhoff boys were born) is in nice contrast to another one 50 years later, when *Babar's Little Girl* Isabelle is born, literally, out in the open like a real elephant baby.

The wholly domestic scenes that follow show that Babar and Céleste revel in parenthood: they graciously receive congratulations and gifts from their subjects, each according to his place in the economy of Célesteville; they easily agree on names, Céleste deciding on "Flora" and Babar on "Pom and Alexander. . . . That's perfect. Let's keep these names" (14), and they both contribute to caring for the little family.

But, like traditional French parents, each has a clearly defined parental role in this gently instructive primer for child rearing. Babar, for example, does not attend the weekly weighing-in, nor does he assist the three women when supplementary feeding— "six bottles of cow's milk, to which you must add a tablespoonful of honey" (15)—becomes necessary. Neither is he in the nursery when Flora nearly chokes on her silver rattle; it is Céleste who finds the baby "purple in the face" and, with textbook aplomb, "grabs her, turns her upside down and shakes her" (17). Throughout the books, Céleste does the physical, at-home nurturing— feeding and washing, preventing or tending sickness, cuddling and wiping tears—in keeping with the important, traditional mother/wife character de Brunhoff has given her.

Father Babar also nurtures his family, but differently—by expanding their experience, in later books through travel and adventure and in this one by playing with them. He and dignified Cornelius, in a double spread posthumously colored by young Laurent, contrast comically with the tiny triplets as they define their masculine relationship to the babies by teaching them books, blocks, and games to make their minds and muscles grow. As times goes on, Babar introduces the children to picnicking and the delights of Lake Céleste, after which the brave diver Babar rescues Alexander from a crocodile and drowning. Obviously a model of participatory, loving fatherhood, Babar nevertheless turns his youngest over to Céleste for "dry clothes . . . hot drinks" (38) and mothering. Both parents find themselves "gradually calming down after all these exciting events" (40) as they remember the hectic day sitting side by side on the parlor couch. But Babar's role in the parenting partnership is clearly distinct from Céleste's, a discrete complementarity that he maintains until Laurent "fathers" Isabelle, a 1987 event that he smilingly admits is not autobiographical.

Arthur and Zephir enjoy being boys as well as men: they play and yet have responsibilities, which they manage with typical adolescent inconsistency. Immediately after the babies' birth, both are "terribly excited [and] walk in quietly [to admire the] tiny . . . cute" (11) newborns. And resourceful Zephir saves Flora from choking, though his mischievous days are far from over. Teenage "Arthur is very glad to be trusted" (20) with walking the triplets but becomes distracted by a passing parade and forgets babies and pram, with near-tragic results. The two will be attentive older brothers to the royal triplets, alternately models of adventure, responsibility, or mischief, never fully maturing.

The babies' personalities are first suggested in this story. "Pom is the greediest and the fattest. . . . He always cries when his bottle is empty" (15). The eldest, he will be the biggest and most aggressive of the three; indeed, in the longer serialized story, big brother Pom has a nighttime adventure of his own. "Flora is very good" (16) as both baby and toddler but is rather timid, even in Laurent's early books, and cries frequently, definitely not the mark of a tomboy or, as yet, a feminist. Alexander, smallest and youngest, is the most adventurous, either by accident or intent. His scary fall into the trees (also colored by Laurent) leaves him undaunted and ready for more mischief with Cornelius's derby hat, which leads to the hair-raising experience with the hungry crocodile. Despite their differences, the siblings look and often dress alike and get along well. They share the nursery, are usually happy to be tucked into their identical beds, and respond affectionately to their parents' loving nurture. Developing their individuality further will be a major focus of Laurent's books.

The elegantly slim Old Lady helps Céleste with cuddling, feeding, and nursing; like Cécile de Brunhoff, she also attends to the children's musical education as she helps the Babars raise their family. Cornelius, a fictional grandfather figure, is not too dignified to let Alexander swing on his aged tusks; Dr. Capoulosse, again a reminder of Grandpère Sabouraud, is as good with babies as with snakebite and burns.

Nor has Babar's personality changed; the ideals he dreamed in *Babar the King* have only been given a new testing ground as he realizes, "Truly it is not easy to bring up a family" (40). He is equal to the task because he has, like Jean de Brunhoff, the requisite for successful fatherhood—love of home and family: "But how nice the babies are! I wouldn't know how to get along without them any more" (40). Babar's family-world is now complete. Indeed, where would Jean take the saga now?

Babar and Father Christmas

This story, written also for the *Daily Sketch* and serialized from 12 November to 23 December 1936, was Jean's last work before his treatment at the Swiss tuberculosis sanatorium where he died the next autumn. Before it could be published as a book, it had to be rewritten, finished from sketches that did not appear in the newspaper version, and colored, again by Michel de Brunhoff with Laurent doing the cover. However, as if to underscore that the story is essentially Jean's despite its final composite authorship, the copyright page of the first French edition declares, "Ce livre a été composé et dessiné par Jean de Brunhoff en octobre novembre 1936" (This book was composed and drawn by Jean de Brunhoff in October/November, 1936), an eerie reminder to 1941 readers of the author's premature death.

De Brunhoff takes Babar on a fairy-tale adventure, one without, however, the imaginative richness of *Zephir's Holidays*. This story's interest comes from plot and a new, fantastic setting rather than from development of Babar's character and utopia. Laurent is sometimes criticized for making Babar a mere observer/adventurer rather than a creative leader; but actually, Jean is the first de Brunhoff to give Babar a weakened role—as a kind of tourist on a mission that he didn't think of first to obtain magical help that is inconsistent with the logic of his world. Unable to add anything new to the elephant king's nature or milieu, Jean could do little but send him abroad.

Different from *The Travels of Babar*, which enriches adventure with personal growth, this story is a series of episodes that the now-familiar Babar goes through. Admittedly, braving the unknown to bring Christmas to Célesteville yields some pleasure, excitement, and expected double spreads. But compared to the innovative vigor of earlier stories and the importance of their events (birth, death, growth to manhood, marriage, career, fatherhood), this adventure seems contrived and the task trivial, even if it does suggest why daddies wear Santa outfits. Understandably, the illness sapping Jean's life was affecting his artistic vitality. But whether he had died or lived, his stories had inevitably to modulate from creating theme and character to making variations on the Babar idea. There was a limit to how much of himself he could put into his fictional elephant king, and he may eventually have shifted from Babar-as-center, as Laurent had to do.

Babar and Father Christmas begins, predictably, at home in the garden. The triplets and Arthur hear an amazing story from Zephir about "a very kind old gentleman with a large white beard, wearing a red suit."[5] Father Christmas lives in "Man's country" (5) and the children are eager for him to leave presents for them, too. The wish lists show their already solidifying personalities: "Flora would love to have a doll. Alexander wants a butterfly net, Pom a big bag of candies. . . . As for Arthur, his dream is to have a train" (9). In due course, Zephir is elected to write Father Christmas a letter, "for he has the best handwriting" (10), which he has diligently learned at Célesteville's excellent school.

But when their daily mail check yields no reply, Babar, always a watchful parent, muses, "Whatever can be the matter with those children? They look so dreadfully sad" (11), as indeed their dejected posture shows. He learns the source of their gloom but reassures them with "cheer up and run along now and play. Possibly you've given me a very excellent idea" (12). At this point, pipe smoking, pacing, and wondering why he didn't think of it himself, Babar decides to invite Father Christmas personally to visit the elephants' land. Leaving Céleste "at home to rule the country during his absence" (13)—and to mother the children and play her usual family role—Babar sets off to find the elusive and, he suspects, shy gift bringer.

Babar pursues Father Christmas with his customary benign logic and aplomb. Leaving Célesteville, he "arrives in Europe"

(13), Paris, of course, complete with French porters, hotel, and Seine-side bookstalls. "In order not to be recognized he has left his crown at home" (13), though why he would hazard losing his identity again is anyone's guess; as an ordinary tourist in a fedora, he checks into a modest pension, the Hotel du Coq Rouge. After settling in, he "washes up a bit. One always feels so refreshed after a good cleaning up" (14), another not-too-subtle reminder of the *gentilhomme*'s proper regime of bodily care. Though the room is quite clean, he is visited by three young mice who address him in a mannerly way and are thrilled to tell him they know where Father Christmas is.

But the mice's attic treasure is disappointing: "I want to find the real live Father Christmas, not a doll!" (17), says Babar sadly. And the search goes on. Some birds lead him to Lazarro Campeotti, an artist's model, but the Father Christmas look-alike cannot help him. A book promises information but neither the hotel manager nor Professor Gillianez can translate it. Even erudite Professor William Jones, with help from a bust of his intellectual mentor Socrates, can tell Babar little more than "Father Christmas . . . lives in Bohemia, not far from the little town of PRJMNESWE" (21) (the text of the serial story has "Przmnbstwe," a curious editorial alteration).

Because Babar's world usually gently satirizes that of men, de Brunhoff makes only one person, the Old Lady, an integral part of it. But this is not Babar's territory, and he meets human beings that Jean has as wryly caricatured as he did in *The Travels of Babar:* Campeotti is appropriately Bohemian and the concierge obsequious with patent-leather hair, moustache, and flashy suit; Professor Gillianez, looking not at all Spanish, has curly red hair, a beard, and professional solidity; balding scholar Jones with pince-nez wears a wing-tip collar and a stuffy formality that contrast with his (tippler's?) red cheeks and nose.

Babar does not, however, seem consistently large in proportion to these people. In Jean's early stories, he grows from a young elephant who is just a little larger than the Old Lady to a full-size pachyderm whose bulk looms much higher and broader than human beings'. Here he is barely taller and fatter than the men—

or than little Virginia and her grandmamma in the park. In the finished book, he is nearly the same size as Father Christmas, perhaps justified by their symbolic equality. But inconsistencies bother children and these are further evidence of the book's bumpy development.

Babar's quest seems impossible until Duck, a homeless dog based on Laurent and Mathieu's beloved "Truffle," offers to help. Having a good sense of smell, he can find lost things and uses the scent of Virginia's Christmas doll to provide the needed clue. The search is on, but not before thankful courtesies are dispensed to Duck and Virginia, who knows there is a Santa Claus! Interestingly, the *Daily Sketch* episode does not name the "little girl" at all; "Virginia" appears only in the book, perhaps the result of other de Brunhoffs' fondness for literary allusions[6] and puns.

The scene changes abruptly from summer garden to Alpine mountain, and the adventure begins in earnest. Fur-hatted Babar and the indispensable dog have a difficult uphill journey through snowy forests, partly by sleigh and partly on skis. Duck is a good scout, though, and gets within distance of a band of red-clad, bearded mountain dwarfs who pelt him with snowballs, get routed by one deep blow from Babar's trunk, and scurry back to tell their master, Father Christmas, about the "enormous animal with a long nose" (29). At this point, the *Daily Sketch* story stops (Wednesday, 23 December 1936). As throughout, the book and serial wording is slightly different, but the picture is the same—of big Father Christmas listening carefully to the little dwarves' report. English children did not, unfortunately, see Babar and Father Christmas get together that year.

But the book continues from drawings that Jean had made, as Babar and Duck struggle onward. "A storm of extraordinary violence suddenly" (30) envelopes them, and they are forced to dig a snow shelter, ingeniously roofed over with Babar's skis. The four-part double spread blizzard is superb: Babar and Duck strive against the fierce wind, buried under a canopy of whirling white flakes against a gray sky, with only Babar's red-scarfed ski pole a sign of their presence. Although these pictures evoke quite a different feeling from the famous mountain skiing double spread of *The Travels of Babar,* the movement and color of the scenes, whoever drew them, offer a thrilling moment of tension—before Babar drops through a hole. "Where have they fallen?" (31).

It is into "the cave of Father Christmas" (32) where, at the hands of the elusive gift bringer and his messenger elves, the half-frozen Babar is rubbed, brandied, and hot-souped until he feels his old courteous self once more. An excellent host and not shy at all, Father Christmas gives a tour of his workshop. Unfortunately, this picture shows its serialized origins; without the intricate, challenging minutiae that Jean would ordinarily have poured into one of his major pictures, the workshop's marvels appear banal when blown up to double-spread book size—heavy-lined generalizations that do no more than repeat the words.

Babar asks his host if he will "distribute toys to the elephant children, just as he does to the children of men" (34, 35). However, when Father Christmas declines because his deliveries in Man's world are too tiring, Babar invites him to "come back with me now to our country and bask in the sun. You will be rested and cured for Christmas" (37). Off they go, not in a flying sleigh full of toys but in Father Christmas's unique transport.

The strange little green vehicle drawn by twelve white birds leaves the snowy north and lands safely in palm-green Céleste-ville, where the travelers are warmly greeted by all the elephants. But especially excited and pleased are the five letter-writing children, who receive courteous introductions to Father Christmas and a promise for a Merry Christmas. After sufficient rest and recovery—riding a zebra while Babar bicycles and taking two-hour sunbaths at Dr. Capoulosse's direction—Father Christmas is ready for home and his Christmas work. But not before he secures his promise to the little elephants by passing his gift-bringing mantle to Babar: "a magic suit which will enable you to fly through the air [and a bag that] will always be full of toys." Father Christmas's own responsibility—and promise—will be to return with "a fine Christmas tree" (40).

How many readers wish that the bottom-quarter-page drawing of red-suited, white-bearded Babar, flying through the star-filled night sky with toys on his back and a stocking in his trunk, were a full-page picture or, better yet, a tour de force de Brunhoff double spread? Laurent used this climactic moment for his cover, but the funny grandeur of lighter-than-air Babar is missed in books with solid-color library bindings. Similarly, the moment when Babar-Santa tiptoes by the sleeping triplets' cribs to deliver toy-filled stockings deserves, but does not get, as much space as the wake-up scene on Christmas morning when the children get more than they asked for. Momentum flounders here; what should be a climactic (even if not especially Babar-worthy) moment—indeed the reason for the whole adventure—is barely a visual footnote. Would Jean, had he seen his story to book, have so minimized the scene?

After real father Babar does his work, legendary Father Christmas keeps *his* promise. The Christmas tree double spread, a family scene curiously without the Old Lady, is bright with color but begs for detail, having also been blown up to book size. The customary treetop star, or for that matter any religious symbolism, is nowhere evident. That this celebration is purely secular (even materialistic, lacking any altruistic message of "Peace on earth" or "Good will to men") should not be surprising, for Jean has introduced no feeling or trappings of religion into the Babars' daily life. There is no church in Célesteville and, though a few distant spires dot rural landscapes, no clergy to tend them. Jean was educated in Protestant schools; Cécile, a Catholic, had the boys baptized into her religion. But beyond that, Laurent says, "neither of them were religious so religion didn't have any real part in our lives." The elephants of Célesteville need only ethics and imagination, not supernatural powers, to sustain their utopia.

However, de Brunhoff clearly wants children to have "faith" in Father Christmas and the magic suit that enables Babar to fly. Why he (or those who saw the book to completion) split the job between Father Christmas and Babar, violated the logic of Célesteville with magic, and ignored any altruistic rationales for Christmas is hard to say. This demystification of Father Christmas forecasts Raymond Briggs's clever books but spoils the enchantment of Christmas morning. If meaning is muddy, text is even less satisfying. Wordy from the beginning, the wooden (at least in translation) prose merely repeats the pictures, and Jean's former delicate, spare counterpoint is gone. Perhaps Babar, whose virtues are earthbound, is, like this story, really too heavy to fly. Would Jean, had he completed the book, have ended this way?

Despite its commercial overtones, *Father Christmas* is ultimately appealing simply because Babar is in it. So sturdy is the elephant king after six well-conceived stories that a seventh, brought to publication without Jean de Brunhoff, does not seriously mar his luster, popularity, or stature as a model adult "human" being.

Posthumous Editions

Babar had become so popular on both sides of the Channel that, in the absence of new books, Jean's old stories were adapted or reprinted; in fact, there was such a reassuring crop of Babars that some readers were not even aware of the creator's death, blaming the paucity of new adventures on the war.

In England, Methuen commissioned the favorite children's writer Enid Blyton to do a small, sparsely illustrated, black-and-white prose retelling of Babar's adventures. Later, Laurent did a similar volume for Hachette in French.[7] Speaking of these wordy paraphrases today, however, Laurent says, "I don't like either of them. . . . I think it was a mistake to try to tell only with words the story of Babar."

In France, and with the justification of "serving the memory of Jean de Brunhoff and responding to the wishes of our young public," Hachette published *Trois "Babar" en un* (1943; *Three "Babars" in One*), a black-and-white reduction from Jean's plates for the first three books; two years later *Deux "Babar" en un* (*Two "Babars" in One*) followed the same format for the last two. There were no editions of *A.B.C. of Babar* and *Zephir's Holidays,* perhaps because Babar was barely evident in both.

Then in 1952 Hachette introduced the "Little Book" concept (reprinted by Methuen as "Little Babar Books") in which each of

Jean's classic stories was cut into pieces, reduced in size, and published under such titles as *L'enfance de Babar (Babar's Childhood)*, *Le couronnement de Babar (Babar's Coronation)*, and *Babar au cirque (Babar at the Circus)*; Laurent expanded and added pictures to some, like *Babar aux sports d'hiver (Babar and Winter Sports)*. None of these adaptations, however, captured the large-size magnificence of the "Big Babars"; instead, they set dubious precedent for future reductions that publishers hoped would touch a broader market than the upper-middle-class one of the original, expensive books.

In America, though Jean de Brunhoff's early "Big Babars" were quickly published by Random House, and Whitman issued a two-volume paperback version of *The Story of Babar* in 1950, Babar was not exactly a household word. Before the 1960s there were few critical evaluations or even reviews of the stories. But with Laurent's adoption of Random House as Babar's *primary* publisher, the elephant king's world became widely known in the United States, still favored by the relatively affluent but issued in affordable editions that targeted ever-younger readers.

Whatever success and popularity Babar stories have today, however, is ultimately due to Jean de Brunhoff's creative genius and fatherly intelligence, bequeathed to a world of readers and, fortunately, to a son who could also make picture books.

4

The Preservation of Babar's World: Laurent de Brunhoff's "Father-Faithful" Stories, 1946–1961

When Laurent de Brunhoff "resurrected" Babar in 1946, he was just 21, a bachelor who wanted to be a painter but was committed also to his father's legacy of making picture books about an elephant utopia. Laurent's career with Babar would be nearly seven times as long as Jean's; his output would be, if not as steady, five times greater. Obviously, in 45 years his perspective, goals, and work would change.

But he began only with the dream of preserving his father's beloved elephant king, as a respectful son who could not have predicted the full implications of his choice. In his first six Babars, with one exception, he contained his own freer artistic impulses and made books that are resolutely as true as possible to Jean's spirit and style. Inevitably there grew a tension between his real self, the painter who strove for originality and self-expression, and his role as the preserver of a tradition. But for 15 years Babar changed very little.

Babar's Cousin: That Rascal Arthur

"Dedicated to the memory of my father, Jean de Brunhoff," *Babar's Cousin: That Rascal Arthur* (*Coquin*, 1946) was greeted by the French as eagerly as the Allies in Paris. So delighted were readers that the benign elephant had survived the war intact, they were scarcely aware of a change in author. And indeed, this adventure seems to pick up smoothly from where Jean's last one left off. The art and literary style are not markedly different and the main personalities introduced by de Brunhoff the elder all appear on the first page of this story. Laurent personally supervised the printing, and except for substandard postwar paper in the French edition, this "Big Babar" brought back the well-loved places, ideas, and quality that had made the saga a national treasure.

"Tired out by a year of hard work"—and five years of war—the Babars set out for a "vacation by the sea."[1] Though Babar and Céleste had gone away to honeymoon and Babar had visited Father Christmas, the trip to Baribarbotton ("It is nice music: *barir* is to trumpet and *barbotter* is to splash in the water," says Laurent) is the first *family* vacation, anticipating later adventures of the royal ménage and Laurent's continuing love of wordplay. Building on Jean's settings but creating new ones too, Laurent will universalize the stories for modern readers and keep the elephant utopia from becoming quaintly archaic or isolated. And because he identified more with teenage Arthur than with fatherly Babar, this story heralds Laurent's preference for younger protagonists.

The adventure begins, though, in the familiar way, with the family waving "Au revoir!" (3) to Cornelius and the old lady, who will presumably keep Célesteville's homefires burning. The group embarks at the station, triplets and Zephir boarding a new mode of travel introduced by Laurent, a "little overhead cable car" (4) while heavier, nearly grown Arthur must "travel with the grown-ups" (5) on the train. The first double spread is well designed and imaginative, but it lacks the visual subplots and minute detail that are so intriguing in Jean's work, another sign of things to come.

Adolescent Arthur can't travel with the other children, but he is still one of them—teasing, reveling in the ocean, and then setting off irresponsibly on his own to explore, only to do more unintentional mischief than ever before. Meanwhile, the rest of the family has a lovely time at the beach: "Pom and Alexander play with their father. They pretend they are little packages and he tosses them about" (9). If Babar is the same participatory father, Céleste is still the traditional mother, always responsive to surroundings—"Oh, how beautiful the sea is!" (7)—and the need "to prepare their afternoon snack" (9). Looking disconcertingly human with his mesomorphic physique, Zephir recalls "Eleanor [sic] the mermaid, and the princess Isabel [sic]" (9, a curious change from the spellings in Zephir's Holidays) for Flora, who dons a pair of crab earrings while her manly brothers fish for shrimp. But except for the brief beach scene, the triplets are not yet individuated in this story, as the title would suggest.

"But where is Arthur?" (11). Typically, that lover of machines has gone in search of "the well-known airport near by. 'Here's something far more interesting than fishing!'" (12). Enthralled by "red planes, blue planes, black planes" (13), he succumbs and climbs into a green one just as it takes off. Some appalled watchers down below rush to tell Babar, while others witness the miraculous rescue-by-trunk as a passenger, defying aerodynamics, pulls Arthur in through a window. Arthur is always brought to account for his mischief, though, and the pilot, "a cranky rhinoceros" (17), possibly a relative of Rataxes, gives him not only a verbal reprimand but, uncharitably, a parachute for bailing out. Even this potential danger is met with great aplomb by the ingenuous teenager who, like Pooh after the honey tree, rather enjoys his descent, "just like a real swing!" (18). This sky-intensive scene predicts the clear color and serene space that will mark Laurent's pictures in the 1980s, and the landing is far less hazardous than Babar and Céleste's unplanned balloon drop in *The Travels of Babar*.

Somehow, Arthur misses his target and instead of falling to "where the Arabs live" (17), he lands in a place incongruously populated by both giraffes and kangaroos, who had been admitted to Babar's kingdom in *A.B.C. of Babar*. Jean's detail is sorely missed in a kangaroo double spread that should imply many separate stories; when compared with the original (Weber, 99), this reproduction seems even stiffer, flatter, and duller. Unfortunately, Laurent's spontaneous painting style is all too often poorly served with printing and, as in this case, the energy of his brush goes unrecognized. Even so, it is a pity that the kangaroo scene is omitted from cheaper, smaller Hachette reprints after 1960— as are interesting double spreads from all of Laurent's first five (and six of Jean's) books.

Boy-man Arthur enjoys his play with three baby kangaroos until a train takes him to his destination—almost. Throughout the adventure, though, "he is worried about what will happen when he gets back, for he will most surely be scolded for having so stupidly climbed up on the plane" (26). Knowing that thoughtless behavior is consistently punished, Arthur has good reason for dread: he has indeed worried his family! Babar even approaches the ill-tempered pilot, not the first time the elephant king has had words with a rhinoceros. "Something serious may have happened to this young man and, if so, it's your fault" (31). Then, like a true gentleman-father armed with appropriate clothing, "his tropical helmet to protect him from sunstroke, a heavy overcoat to keep him warm on cold nights" (31), Babar heads for El Talahil and, he hopes, Arthur.

Meanwhile, Arthur has found a means of transportation even more interesting than train—two dromedaries who, with the help of some hippos, kindly carry him over a crocodile-infested river. Dromedaries and hippos danced at Babar's wedding and are worthy animals in Babar's kingdom and Leach's hierarchy; but crocodiles are unregenerate villains in all the Babars! The dromedaries, twins in form and movement, carry Arthur through the desert day and protect him at night until they reach an oasis village, complete with adobe houses, curious Arabs (familiar figures from *A.B.C. of Babar*), and a primitive well.

No sooner has the parched adolescent "had two pails of water, full to the brim" (41) than he sees Babar coming down the street. "They embrace each other heartily. What joy to be reunited at last! But . . . the time has come for a scolding" (42). Laurent sounds like vintage Jean here—the loving warmth, the call to personal responsibility, the courteous grace of "thanking the dromedaries warmly for their kindness" (42), and concern about Céleste, who "is upset about you" (43).

The reunion is capped with food (always a high point!) at the home of Babar's old friend, Moustapha, an affluent Arab who hosts the elephants in a spaciously exotic room, red floored and white walled, with an enticing cul-de-sac divan. They eat a pleasing array of "oranges and bananas and delicious honey cakes called 'gazelles' horns'" (44, 45), sitting cross-legged on the floor and reveling in the bonhomie. This time Laurent's preference for uncluttered design over intricate detail captures perfectly the mood of the leisurely meal, its indoor cool contrasted with the outdoor heat.

Well rested, the travelers return home in Babar's new caterpillar "tractor" (46), obviously inspired by the desert-tested World War II tanks that made obsolete warriors of cavalry—and dromedaries. They arrive back at Baribarbotton to an excited reception from Céleste, the triplets, and Zephir. But Arthur, too tired from exhilaration even to undress, is unaware of Céleste's tender candlelight ministrations, "She is very, very happy to have him back again" (48).

And so Laurent ends his first story, striking the expected chord of security-after-adventure that is the saga's hallmark and his legacy. Under close scrutiny, one can see emerging personal differences despite Laurent's desire to be "very faithful." But the tone and substance are authentic Babar, and death and war have not disrupted this family.

Babar's Picnic

At a new home, Babar's "country place near Celesteville,"[2] the family and their guest, old General Cornelius, enjoy waking up to beautiful mornings in the garden. In *Babar's Picnic* (*Pique-nique,* 1949) readers see for the first time another Babar residence, which, like Chessy, provides rural respite from their city house.

Right from the start, the children are in charge; it is their picnic, not Babar's, making the English title *Picnic at Babar's* (Methuen, 1950) more accurate than the American. Zephir organizes, Arthur, now old enough to chauffeur, consults an intriguing map of the kingdom, and the three little ones pack playthings. Some adventures slow their departure: trips down the curving banister for the boys; a venture to the market for Flora, who is too cautious for banister sliding but brave enough for her maiden voyage to the market alone to buy "cakes for the picnic" (8); and a rescue by Arthur when the tiny elephant gets lost in the marketplace crowd, all episodes that reinforce the children's emerging personalities and the interesting world they live in.

Finally, though, they are ready, and Babar gives his parental admonition, "And remember, no nonsense. Be good!" (10). The picnickers motor to a lovely valley spot to settle into their games, chess for the old compatriots Arthur and Zephir and a game of Indians for the little ones. When the lively boys argue over who is leader, Flora shows pacifying tact, "Listen! I know, we'll all three be chiefs!" (11).

The "Indian chiefs" wear the headdress of American Indians but the same leaf skirts, bare-topped except for Flora's pearls, as the "fierce and savage cannibals" in *The Travels of Babar.* The children are, in fact, in the country of "natives" (*nègres* in *Piquenique,* 10) who don't eat elephants but are quaintly primitive, superstitious, and live in "funny houses" (19). These pseudo-Negroid human beings that Laurent alternately calls "nègres" and "sauvages" (but not "cannibales" like Jean's "sauvages") look disturbingly like the prominent-mouthed, noseless monkeys of *Zephir's Holidays.* In fact, when an anxious Zephir finally "discovers Pom, Flora and Alexander among some savages" (17), he could be back in Monkeyville among his own kind!

Though unintentional, the portrait of minorities, especially blacks, is insensitive and was ultimately unacceptable to editors at Random House. Laurent, embarrassed at his unconscious racism, withdrew *Babar's Picnic* from publication in the early 1960s. The affinity with Jean's 1930s concept of blacks perhaps partly owes to Laurent's well-intentioned faithfulness to his father's work, partly to his racially homogeneous, bourgeois milieu. Whatever the reason, though the intervening action and pictures are vigorous, today's readers are relieved when the triplets escape from the jungle village.

A storm comes up, forcing the five to rush for shelter, amid fierce wind and lashing rain. Provident Arthur makes sure all are in dry clothes, secures the tent, and, snugly battened down, they have a fine time—until, "Hey! The water is coming into the tent" (30). The adventurers find themselves in the middle of a flood! Arthur falls into a hole and would drown but for quick-thinking Zephir and cooperative siblings: "Just one more pull, all together!" (33). The children indeed know how to work as well as play. Naturally, Zephir is ready with the appropriate handkerchief and candid sartorial advice to his soaked friend, "You'll have to change your clothes this evening. You look disgusting" (34). But "can they start the car . . . after it has gotten so drenched? Impossible!" (34), and, in a picture that falls short of Laurent's lively original idea (Weber, 110), their old marabou friends tow them back home.

Once there, they find that Célesteville, too, is flooded, and all the elephants are cruising the watery green landscape in boats. The children get rescued by Babar, kissed by Céleste, and the car is towed to the mechanic's, thanks to General Cornelius. At home after dinner, Babar and Cornelius play billiards like the de Brunhoffs and Sabourauds at Chessy. But when Céleste announces bedtime, three tired but obedient children in dressing gowns "go without waiting to be told a second time" (40), doubtless happy to be dry and safely back home.

Once again, secure images of home and family bracket hair-raising adventures; reminders of optimism, courtesy, cooperation, persistence, work, and play pervade the story. There are almost too many episodes one after another, but Laurent's narrative is pleasantly varied if a little wordy, perhaps partly the fault of an English translation that is even less direct and economical than the French: "Une première fois lentement!" (Pique-nique, 7) becomes the more cumbersome "Take it easy, try it slowly the first time" (7). Thus the effect in some places is of more script than illustration.

Visual detail is still wanting, particularly in the market scene, though in the flood double spreads Laurent's splashy style is effective. His talent for showing movement is clear in the hunt dance, which is alive with, albeit unacceptable, ritual frenzy, and in the lashing, chilly rainstorm. Colors in reproduction seem more garish than Laurent's original, carefully chosen greens, yellows, and reds; considering all the watery moments, however, blue is sorely missed, even more than in *The Story of Babar* and *Babar the King*. This is particularly true of reproductions other than the superb French first edition printed by Gaston Maillet et Cie of St. Ouen (who would print three more of Laurent's "Big Babars"), which makes up somewhat for blue with its velvety blacks, subtly varied greens, and pinks.

Readers learn a little more about the youngsters: Arthur is brave and responsible, if accident-prone; Zephir is intelligent and resourceful; Pom is chubby and boisterous; Flora is feminine, gentle but strong, brave, and tactful; Alexander is still the littlest. It is unfortunate that an explainable but indefensible lack of racial sensitivity has made this book virtually obsolete. Laurent did, however, redraw the rainstorm for *Isabelle's New Friend* (1991), giving new life to one of his favorite pictures.

Babar's Visit to Bird Island

On his first visit to America, Laurent admitted, "If I were an animal I would like to be a bird,"[3] not, as one might expect, an elephant. Indeed, he has poured himself into this visually dazzling book, which celebrates "birdness" with all the skill and energy of a talented painter. His family's favorite, it is the most individual work of this early period and "very special" to him. His elephants are still rotundly controlled, but the other lines—in birds, sailboats, ocean waves, flowers—are joyously freer than in any books in his "father style" and more exuberant than he will be again.

In *Babar's Visit to Bird Island* (*Ile aux oiseaux,* 1951) Laurent creates a new environment, but typically, the royal triplets start from home, Arthur and Zephir having slept late, for a walk along the riverbank. There they meet "three birds in a sailboat; two . . . that look like cranes, with beautifully colored plumage, and a little green duck,"[4] who are eager to find King Babar. The stunning visitors are "Piros and Cardombal, ambassadors of the King of the Birds" (7); Babar welcomes them graciously and eagerly accepts their king's invitation "to visit their island" (8).

The family loses no time in embarking—Pom and Alexander on the birds' backs, Flora in the safer sailboat with the duck, and Babar and Céleste with Cornelius in the royal yacht. The airborne pair have a spectacular bird's-eye view as they approach the island, nicely foreshadowing their adventures and receive a stunning landing reception "surrounded by a tremendous display of whirling birds that look almost like fireworks" (12). The double-spread introduction to adventure is magnificent with color— intense blues, oranges, greens—and sweeping energy.

The others land in a more mundane way, whereupon each is ceremoniously outfitted in "a beautiful feather costume" (15). Reminiscent of *Babar the King,* a portrait page wittily introduces some of the Bird Islanders, whose occupations fit admirably their bird natures: feather-crowned King Cyprian and Queen Ursula, the deep-billed Pelican Postman, bright-plumed Pheasant Tailors, flambuoyant Parrot and Peacock, "who are actors" (17), leggy Dancing Crane, Vulture Butcher, and the rest.

Finally the elephants meet island royalty. King Cyprian leads them through a jungle "forest of strange trees and plants" (18), past Queen Ursula inappropriately taking a shower, to the double-spread hub of island industry, the beehives. Here sinuous, tuba like flowers, all but engulfing the visitors, yield nectar for honey, which is eventually made into gingerbread by pelicans inventively "using their bills as molds" (22). The children are intrigued by the process; after sampling the honey cordial, Babar pronounces the island "enchanting" (23) and the visit delightful.

Abruptly a self-important rooster announces a "big event at the ostrich race track" (26), and the visitors are given ringside seats at what is apparently the community event of the year. The first-lap double spread is disappointingly static, but the finish is breathless, as the little duck passes the rooster to the cheers of "cranes, parrots, pink flamingos, ducks, pelicans, storks, birds of every color" who swirl and cry shrilly, "Hurray! Bravo! Let's carry him in triumph!" (31).

"Surrounded by a tremendous display of whirling birds that look almost like flowers, the two little elephants don't quite know where to look first."

"What a wonderful reception!" says Alexander. "Flora made a big mistake in choosing to go by boat with the little green duck."

Pom and Alexander fly over Bird Island. From *Babar's Visit to Bird Island* by Laurent de Brunhoff. Copyright © 1961 by Laurent de Brunhoff. Reprinted by permission of Random House, Inc.

The shy little duck, surprisingly not named Dog, slips away with Flora. "They feel like going out for a sail" (32) in the clear blue sea—but not before Flora, whom Laurent is steadily making braver, has overcome any timidity about flying on a bird's back like her brothers. "Now she too knows what fun it is to fly" (33). The peaceful outing ends rudely when a huge fish on Flora's line nearly swallows the duck; six pictures capture the calm-to-chaos adventure with exciting economy, showing Laurent once again to be a master of motion and white space.

Happily, just as he had when the crocodile nearly ate Alexander in *Babar and His Children,* Babar comes to the rescue in his gorgeous red sailboat; the fish is netted, Flora is cuddled by Céleste, and the dazed little duck is revived. Under lanterns glinting from shadowy trees, the grown-ups have a fine evening feast on "the wicked fish" (39). "And now it is time to go home" (40). The Babars sail against a starry sky as Piros, Cardombal, and the little duck watch sadly, trusting that they will meet again—which they do. Serenity yet *tristesse* close a day full of mutual discovery.

What makes this book exceptional is not plot, which is undramatically episodic, or character development, though Flora shows new mettle. Nor is it theme, even if tolerance, courtesy, and cooperation are hinted at. *Babar's Visit to Bird Island* is memorable for its imaginative setting, executed with uninhibited, painterly power and wit. For the first time since he saved Babar from oblivion, Laurent shows his originality and a flash of the independence that will surface a decade later; minute detail is compensated for by energy, color, and motion. *"Bird Island* is really one of my favorites. It was the perfect expression of my resentment, my revolt against my father. After that I didn't mind so much being very classic to the tradition" and remaining Jean-faithful for a few more years.

Babar's Fair

Laurent creates another new environment in *Babar's Fair (Fête,* 1954), this time a kind of anniversary celebration and World's Fair on the "far side of [Célesteville's] lake."[5] Free, loose line is not as evident as in *Babar's Visit to Bird Island,* but pictures are packed with inventive ideas and detail; several memorable double spreads, almost Jean-like in their detail, may explain its choice as a *New York Times* Best Illustrated Book in 1956. Indeed, the "many attractions / trips to the bottom of the lake / display of lights" promised on the title page are realized with originality in one of Laurent's best domestic settings.

The title picture hints also that the five youngsters will be the adventurers, for though King Babar, with the help of his living-room cabinet and "dear friends" General Cornelius, Doctor Capoulosse, and Podular the sculptor, organizes and executes the fête, the children have the most fun exploring it.

From the first announcement of "plans and preparations," the elephants of Célesteville "talked of nothing else" (4, 5). The main street hums with activity as citizens pedal, drive, or walk to work, market, or classes; the royal children "were so excited that they almost forgot to go to school" (5). Background shops and signs, still bearing their French names in the American translation— *livres* (books), *épicerie* (grocery store), *tabac* (tobacco), *arrêt* (stop!)—offer, like Jean's *A.B.C. of Babar,* a new glimpse of the city (4, 5). But the focus is on a newspaper kiosk with wryly punning Babarian reading matter—"Trompe et corne" (trunk and horn), "Etudes et jeux" (studies and games), "Les aventures du capitaine Hop LaLa," Zephir's favorite story—where "special editions of the newspapers" are being sold. Pleasant flurry and immediacy move the illustration. Unfortunately, the text is in past tense, a puzzling lapse in translating consistency with other Babars and with the third scene, which springs back to the vital, participatory present.

Animals in the countryside are intrigued by a skywriting announcement: "The Celesteville Fair! Big Exposition! King Babar invites you. Ask for details! Come One! Come All!" (6, 7). Delegates from far-flung countries arrive to register, even Mr. Ramatur, the Envoy Extraordinary from Babar's old enemy, the rhinoceroses. When the big day finally arrives, "an enormous throng" (10) inches past cheering onlookers; led by the slightly apprehensive impressario in a snappy new blue car, they cross the grand elephant bridge, inspired by a real span at Tancarville in Normandy, to the fairground and a new view of developing Célesteville. After a touching speech—"May we all get to know and like each other"—Babar cuts the ribbon and "the fair is open" (14).

Each country had its species-appropriate building: the kangaroos' needs no stairs because "they just hop from floor to floor" (15); the rhinos' is squat but crowned with impressive tusks; the giraffes' is a tall-towered "beautiful castle" (18); the lions' is royally columned and monumented. The birds' exhibit flutters with color and motion, while the monkeys' is alive with ladder climbers. As they move through the attractions, the children meet old friends—the little green duck, King Cyprian and Queen Ursula from Bird Island, Madame Cesarine the giraffe, Barbacol the tailor, Olur the mechanic-turned manufacturer—and make new ones like "a little lion . . . who also is very fond of cakes" (23) and has parents as strict as theirs. Even staid Cornelius forms a lasting relationship with two good conversationalists.

The heart of the fête, where all nations meet, is "the market place under the big dome" with "wonderful things to eat! [and] wonderful things to see!" (20). The busy double spread is packed with irresistible sensory temptations, each booth having some characteristic speciality: the monkeys' has pastries; the giraffes', fruits; the birds', feather-clothing; the dromedaries, camping gear; the lions', sculptures; the rhinos', a model car; and Babar's, his private airplane. Pom especially loves the hippos' "merveilleuses saucisses" (marvellous sausages), and everyone at the market finds something to buy.

Knowledge and experience grow, too: Alexander learns about giraffe country; Pom discovers the difference between a camel and a dromedary; after watching a thrilling play, the children all see the backstage complexities of a kangaroo puppet theater. And with the adults, they have a diving adventure that begins on the still, blue-green of the lake floor but gains tension when "the rascal, Alexander" (29) is nearly drowned.

Later, the animals mingle internationally again, "chatting excitedly" (32) under little tables with yellow umbrellas. Babar and Céleste take "tea" in liqueur glasses with the hippo and lion; other adults enjoy wine as well as lemonade, the candid assumption being that adults can sip what they like: giraffes share an ingenious table and the little duck is just one of the children. The day's success culminates spectacularly under the stars, in a double spread that captures its chilly, exhilarating climax. This nighttime view from the bridge provides a stunning symmetry with its daytime counterpart and a similar feeling of, "What a beautiful city" (13).

After a month of trade and harmony, "the fair is over" (38) and the visitors go home, full of international accord, promises of more fairs, and suitcases bulging with gifts. At home with the little green duck (who disappears from the stories after this), Babar's children relive the unity of the fair at Célesteville as they play lion, giraffe, hippo, and bird.

Like *Babar's Visit to Bird Island,* this story has no narrative climax; setting, conveyed mostly in pictures, *is* plot, as the animals move from one inventive page to the next. Character traits are confirmed: Babar's benevolence, Pom's gourmandise, Alexander's accident-proneness, Flora's tenderness, and Arthur's emerging dependability. The literary strong point of *Babar's Fair* is, however, is its theme, not intentionally didactic but more than accidentally timely as the United Nations struggled for effectiveness in a war-damaged world. Although not as obviously as Jean's books, this story nevertheless reflects the concerns of a man who matured during a great war. Laurent says, "My own wartime feelings don't appear in my books, except perhaps as a reaction against war in *fête de Célesteville,* which was a *réunion internationale pacifique!*" Indeed, if elephant and rhinoceros can trade and eat together, Laurent de Brunhoff suggests, the human community can coexist peacefully, not just by arms control in a newly formed NATO but by commerce in a European Economic Community. From a man who determinedly avoids overt messages in his stories, this is strong stuff.

Babar and the Professor

Babar and the Professor (*Professeur,* 1956), the last of Laurent's "Big Babars," is a visual tour de force, introducing a mysterious underground world and adventures for the extended Babar family. Two new characters, inspired by Laurent's own children Anne and Antoine, temporarily take Zephir's place as playmates for the young elephants. And an Einstein-looking, butterfly-chasing intellectual takes over from Babar—for the first time but with the elephant king's approval—as the adult with ideas. The story was written in 1954 and published the next summer as a weekly series in the Hachette-owned French magazine *Elle;* Laurent adapted some of the pictures for the book format and still considers it "one of my best."

Sitting in his garden, "living happily in Celesteville," Babar reads a letter announcing that the Old Lady, her brother Professor Grifaton, and his two grandchildren, Nadine and Colin, will be visiting. "What wonderful news!"[6] Driving a Volkswagen, the guests arrive to a double-spread welcome in which the bulky, affectionate elephants all but envelop the slender visitors.

But the children are a little tentative, especially domineering Pom, and when they all go to bed, he is so "furious" at Colin's "rough-housing" that he "catches the little fellow by the foot and whirls him around faster and faster," making his poor head spin almost explosively. In loyal sisterly fashion Nadine plunges in, "Don't you dare hurt my brother!"; Flora and Alexander rush to rescue Colin; and finally Babar has to intervene "sternly." Laurent's children show, by facial expression and body movement, typical youthful reaction to novelty, overexcitement, and temper; there had been a sibling squabble in *Picnic,* and his future stories will accept bickering as a normal part of childhood relationships, to be recognized and dealt with. A new father himself when this was written, Laurent may have had a fresh interest in youthful behavior. In any event, the episode clears the air, and Pom, oldest and biggest, has a lesson in self-control.

He forgets the very next day when they go butterfly hunting, but this time Colin is an ally in lighthearted mischief. They are all fascinated by the Professor's collapsible butterfly case, engineering charts, books, and microscope. But suddenly Nadine, who has been exploring, calls "Come quick! I've just made a wonderful discovery!"

The cave she leads them to opens a whole new world of possibilities. They create a playhouse, complete with cleverly suspended lanterns and candelabra, invite the adults to tea, and stage a grand costume party. Laurent's underground pictures are darkly whorled with potential passages, and tea is sumptuous, "a fine feast with lots of cakes" including Arthur's favorite éclairs. The costume double spread is not so detailed as Jean's sartorial promenade in *Babar the King,* but large-footed Professor Grifaton in top hat, Cornelius in Restoration wig, Flora in hoopskirt, chunky Pom as Mercury, and Colin as a little devil reveal Laurent's wit and sense of incongruity at its best. Not as fond of costume as Jean, here he is faithful to his father in his own fashion.

Adventurous Alexander decides to explore but falls in the dark tunnel and cries for rescue. As in *Babar's Fair,* the littlest triplet, well-lit by flashlight crossbeams and comforted by Cousin Arthur, is hauled up by his trunk, to the relief of worried adults. It is indeed a theatrical moment and Alexander basks in the center stage.

Babar is fascinated by the cave and "organizes a group to go down and explore" its depths. Accompanied by familiar Céleste-villians Olur, Podular, "Dr. Capoulosse who goes along in case he might be needed," and Arthur—all appropriately dressed in waterproof overalls and miners' hats—the elephants descend into the murky, "strange-looking forest" of the cave floor. Besides stalactites, they discover "a subterranean river," all of which excites Babar to have Hatchibombotar and Pilophage bring six rubber rafts that navigate the watery passages in a powerfully eerie double spread. "They glide along among the stalactites and the dim vaulted arches" that reveal the ultimate surprise, "the statue of the King of the Mammoths," hulking reminder of the elephants' ancient history. Their dramatic exploration a success, they are surprised to find themselves back in familiar territory, the reedy backwaters of Lake Céleste.

If Babar is intrigued with the grotto, Professor Grifaton, who has joined the raft expedition, is galvanized by its possibilities. With Babar's consent and some technical help, the Professor engineers construction of an excursion steamer so that all the elephants can see their underground heritage. "Conceived and designed by Professor Grifaton," and "propelled by atomic engines with side paddle-wheels," the blueprint is ingeniously complete with A and B decks, ample facilities for shopping, storing supplies, eating, and a unique, if puzzling, combination "Bar and Library."

The maiden trip is sold out, tickets being reasonably priced, and Célesteville families, among them Professor Grifaton in a cowboy hat, pour excitedly onto the red-and-white decks. This quayside double spread, reminiscent of *The Travels of Babar*, clarifies a basic principle of Babarian economics: a healthy capitalism, not a welfare state, prevails, and people do pay to play.

But the children, caught up in their own pleasures and pains, almost miss the trip. Luckily, they are on the bridge when the steamer passes under and can climb safely down a ladder in time for a small boat's descent into the damp subterranean depths. Boat lights illuminate the cavern differently from the lantern-lit raft trip, as awed elephant tourists see beneath their city for the first time.

The enterprise is such a success that "Cornelius decorates Professor Grifaton as Benefactor of Celesteville" at a splendid royal presentation ceremony, complete with Céleste in a Norman Hartnell dress, while the children watch on television with their favorite babysitter, the Old Lady. When departure day arrives, the Professor drives off with Colin and Nadine, promises to return soon, and leaves his sister at home with her elephant family.

Babar and the Professor presents familiar themes: courtesy, when as a guest the Old Lady brings "presents for all of them"; parental consistency, when Babar and Céleste both reprimand the children for bad behavior; balanced work and play; and the value of learning. Characters are confirmed: "big fat Pom" is awkward in size and sometimes in personality; Flora is nurturing, feminine, and "gently blows on [Nadine's knee] to ease the pain"; Alexander is curious, which sometimes gets him in trouble.

But like *Babar's Visit to Bird Island* and *Babar's Fair*, the main focus is setting, principally the cave and its wonders, though Célesteville's above-ground face is subtly changing too, with the former fairground now a suburb of houses and factories. Darkness, which Laurent introduced in the double-spread night tableau of *Babar's Fair,* reaches new importance here, as the story builds to climactic scenes in the cave. Movement is not necessary, for color and scale capture perfectly the tension of these dramatic pictures. Though Laurent intended no ominous symbolism, his stunning black-background illustrations do signal a departure from his father's mostly pastel scenes and another flexing of his own painterly muscle. While he is expanding Célesteville, he is reaching beyond Jean's Babarian world.

A tue-tête

"To fight for my own self and to contain Babar a bit," Laurent explored completely new territory in *A tue-tête* (At the top of one's voice, 1957), a book of satirical caricatures for adults that was not published in English. The witty and virtually untranslatable six-page text that Laurent invited Jacques Lanzman to write is independent of the black-and-white line drawings, making essentially two satires under one cover.[7] The keenly urbane portraits were such a success in France that the French weekly *L'Express* wanted Laurent to draw a series parodying current political figures; though he could have used the income at the time, he preferred to keep his burlesques universal—which these definitely are.

Using a spare, backgroundless style that anticipates his non-Babar stories, Laurent mocks human pretentions with an exquisitely sharp eye and pen. Expressive two-legged human bodies topped with blasé animal heads share the burden of satire. "Mondanités" (social events), first of five sections, captures the controlled enthusiasm of an upper-crust concert audience (like some Cécile and Thierry de Brunhoff must have known) and the comfortable tedium of a post performance white-tie reception. In "les bigotes pompes funèbres" (sanctimonious funerals), an almost-angry denunciation of what he sees as religious hypocrisy, Laurent draws corteges followed by perfunctory mourners for whom the occasions seem mainly social. "Jardin public" (public garden) is a sort of Stages of Man, with lovers, babies, matrons, and hairless old "birds" side by side in eloquent activity. "Les arts et les artistes" (the arts and artists) is especially trenchant as Laurent satirizes his own world of coy model, serious museumgoer, Mona Lisa, Picasso—and dancing camel-man painter who becomes Picardee 30 years later (in *Babar's Little Girl*) but here signs himself "Brunhoff."

Though heads are often from Babar animals, Laurent plays with their meanings: one crocodile is a George Raft–looking masher, another is protective lover, and yet another an intense pipe-smoking painter; the birds are gossips, fashion plates, and art critics; rhinos have political arguments; and lady camels wear false eyelashes and fur coats. De Brunhoff's line is economical and confident; his wit is sharp; his "Thinker" is a fine figure of a man, a statue bird unable, however, to prey. In this "escape from Babar," Laurent shows a new perspective and style, some of which will find its way into other books, eventually even into the Babars.

Babar's Castle

The first Babar published after Hachette's reduction edict, *Babar's Castle* (*Château*, 1961) was written for the 32-page, approximately 9-by-11-inch format that would henceforth be the standard size of Hachette's first-edition mainstream books. Dimensions would vary slightly with reprintings, but, except for facsimiles published in the 1980s, the 10½-by-14½-inch "Big Babars" were obsolete. The American edition, slightly smaller at approximately 8 by 11 inches, was lettered by hand rather than written in the original round script; soon after, at teachers' and librarians' urging, all U.S. editions were machine printed, script being illegible to young American readers. Laurent de Brunhoff eventually agreed to all these publisher-mandated changes—but reluctantly. Indeed, the loss of size and script seriously affect the books' quality.

To reverse the old adage, in this story Babar's ancestral castle is his home, temporarily at least, as he leaves the house in Célesteville "to live in Castle Bonnetrompe."[8] The world is not imaginative like *Babar's Visit to Bird Island* or *Babar's Fair* as, for the first time, Laurent uses an archetypal French reality as his entire setting. The architecture of Jean's Célesteville had come partly from Versailles; Laurent had remembered a market in Rome when he drew *Babar's Picnic* and a bridge in Normandy when he did *Babar's Fair*. But here the story is a guided tour through a château, slightly seedy, in the Dordogne region of southwestern France, with plot again secondary to setting.

The moving van is already unloading as the Babars' luggage-laden green station wagon climbs the castle road, a rural double spread similar in feeling to Babar's first time at the wheel in *The Story of Babar*. Characteristically, the turreted castle dominates a village below and the slow, old river curls through a pastoral French landscape. Inside, "in the impressive entrance hall" (9) common to all châteaux, the children admire portraits of distinguished ancestors, a "handsome musketeer" (9), an Elizabethan lady, and even a Roman soldier.

But the old building needs new plumbing, plaster, and wallpaper. The children help, using their trunks in new ways, all, that is, except curious Alexander who goes exploring for an underground passage. They manage to get dirty enough for Céleste to chide them, "Oh! What a mess! Go take a shower . . . and scrub yourselves with a brush" (11). Clean once more, they join the adults in "the big dining hall" (12), complete with tapestry, huge fireplace, mullion-patterned floor, and massive trestle table (a memory from Chessy?) laden with good French watercress soup and wine. Uncharacteristically, Pom is too tired from his wallpaper exertions to eat.

But he is awake enough when, "in the middle of the night," Alexander leads them all to "look for the underground passage" (14). They "prowl about the castle" (14), climb the tower into the silver-blue light, and meet an owl. Once more Laurent risks comparison with Jean as mood and colors evoke Zephir's silver-light meeting with the nightingale. This treatment of night is unusual for Laurent, whose darkness ordinarily dazzles with color, but the muted textlessness is quietly effective.

The owl does not know of the elusive passage but takes them to the armory, full of heraldic shields and "armor and weapons from the Middle Ages" (16). Arthur in "marvelous gilded . . . armor" (16) and Pom in a "small black suit" (17) have a clanging swordfight until they get tired; Pom cannot remove his boot and must wear it till Babar can come to the rescue.

In a comically formal double spread of a standard château garden, kingly Babar, crowned and suited on his rider-mower La Merveilleuse, happily tends grass that is fringed by topiary trees, an elephant fountain, and geometric flowerbeds, reminiscent of the Tuileries and Jean's *A.B.C. of Babar*. Céleste and the Old Lady chat, Flora catches a goldfish, helpful Arthur rakes, and Zephir, always "up to mischief" (21) carves his initials into a tree.

Finally, inquisitive Alexander "discovers a little building" (22), clearly a typical château *pavilion* (summer house), set amid clipped hedge and satyr-elephant statues at the edge of the equally typical woods. Inside a dark, cobwebby room "full of dusty books" (23), the children finally find the secret tunnel, and, armed with candles, "they cautiously advance in single file. Then they come to a trap door (24). But instead of maximizing the climax with a separate picture, Laurent chooses humor over tension in an above-and-below-ground cross section of garden and basement, perhaps like the one at Chessy, which deliciously frightened Laurent as a child. The children emerge safely from what might have been, but wasn't, an exciting underground adventure, into "the living room of the castle" (25), surprising Babar and Céleste but not the reader. The episode is a little more dramatic in the original French, with some tension and an expletive—"A-A-A-A-lexandre!" (*Château*, 25)—but the picture still gives away too much.

The climax of the château tour is a housewarming party on "the steps of the grand staircase" (27) and in the ballroom. Old friends arrive in furs, top hats, and wonderful cars—Triumphs, Peugeots, a Rolls Royce with a winged-elephant hood symbol—to be greeted by the royal couple in full regalia. The party is a celebration of *croque-en-bouche,* pink champagne, and dancing, with the Old Lady at the piano like Cécile de Brunhoff; even the children are there, the triplets in new party clothes and Arthur and Zephir in their first long pants! "The party continues merrily until dawn" (30), long after the children have gone to bed. The château "under the pale starlit sky" (30) is an austere beacon crowning the hillside, not perhaps as welcoming as in its morning pinkness, but warm inside—and home!

Not especially strong in theme, plot, or character, this story is enlivened by Laurent's eye for funny, colorful incongruity—portrait elephants in period costumes, Pom as the Black Knight, Babar on the mower, elephant couples dancing minuets and waltzes—and his visual punning, opening on the title page with the elephant gardener using his good trunk (*bonne trompe*) as a hose, and closing with another an elephant using *his* good trunk to play what readers hope is good trumpet (also *bonne trompe*)—all at Castle Bonnetrompe!

Laurent had drawn a recognizable Volkswagen in *Babar and the Professor;* here he brings other true-to-life cars into an environment that is central to the story but is transformed very little by fantasy. He does not like the results, much preferring to invent imagined transport and places, like a tractor-jeep, a graceful, high-powered red yacht, a fair, or an underground river. Besides, he says, Babar is too big for a closed-in Citroën DS 10, even one with Paris plates, fitting much better the open red roadster that Jean "borrowed" from dashing de Brunhoff uncles. And the egalitarian monarch is ultimately more comfortable at home in Célesteville, which has no realistic counterpart, than in even a newly decorated castle.

This story, produced at a professional crossroads for Laurent, seems labored. He was outgrowing Jean's Babar mold at the same time that his publisher seemed to be throwing it away. Finding a new direction and outlet for his creativity—and a secure living for his family—was imperative and, for a while, problematic.

5

Experimentation with Babar's World
Laurent de Brunhoff's Stories, 1961–1972

The need to assert his individuality—and to support his young family at a time when the future of Babar was uncertain—prompted Laurent to interrupt the creation of traditional Babar stories temporarily and to experiment—not always successfully—with new subjects, forms, and professional liaisons. During this decade, Laurent forged bonds with American publishers who gave him freedom to create non-Babar stories and move away from Jean-faithful Babar formats. So occupied did he become that he stopped personal painting. and, with that, made the fiscally important career decision to concentrate on creating books for children.

The Serafina Stories

When Laurent approached Georges Borchardt in Paris about publishing *A tue-tête* in America, the literary representative for World Publishing Co. (and de Brunhoff's agent since moving to the United States) thought it unsalable but suggested that he do something for children. The Serafina stories are Laurent's first juvenile non-Babars published in the United States—indeed, published anywhere—a trilogy that chronicles the summer adventures of the first de Brunhoff female protagonist and her four friends.[1]

The drawing style was unexpected from a de Brunhoff, especially for American readers who did not know *A tue-tête*. But even without elephants, this departure from the Babar picture tradition is still markedly Babar-derivative in its plot, character development, and themes. Not works of great originality or Laurent's best "emancipation" stories, the Serafinas still have a certain gentle charm and gave him a springboard for later, more distinguished departures from his father's legacy.

In a Babarian opening, *Serafina the Giraffe* (1961) leaves home on a green train to visit Grandmother Giraffe for her birthday. The need to supply a special cake for the occasion takes Serafina and her friends Patrick the rabbit, Hugo the kangaroo, Beryl the frog, and Ernest the crocodile through a series of misadventures that reveal interesting relationships between the characters and eventually accomplish the task at hand.

First Serafina and then the car get stuck; Beryl falls off a treetop "Eiffel" tower, and Ernest gets hurt while wrestling a suddenly appearing black crocodile; a cake finally gets made—but burned—and only with Lady Rhinoceros's friendly intervention does the party come off and make Grandmother Giraffe "so happy she almost cries." Throughout, characters develop as distinct individuals who alternately argue and make up, tease and help one another—and are more rambunctious than children in most Babars except perhaps for Pom and Colin in *Babar and the Professor*. Serafina is gawky, tenderhearted, and a little scatterbrained; Hugo is a competent leader, Patrick lively and funny, Ernest strong and reliable, and Beryl faithful and brave. Serafina's parents and Grandmother Giraffe with her pince-nez are, like Babar adults, loving but not permissive. The only villain, a "bad" crocodile, is vanquished by the good croc, Ernest, with the help of friends whose personalities give the activities zest.

The flat green, orange, yellow, and brown pictures—hand-separated by Laurent—seem, however, almost careless and scrawly, lacking his accustomed movement and detail. There is no anxiety when semi-comatose Beryl lies limp in her hospital bed, no intensity when the crocodiles fight; the cakes in the *pâtisserie* window are bland reprises of earlier Babar sweet treats. There is some visual humor: Serafina's mother has pearls and her father a bow tie on their long necks; Grandma bends creakily to give Serafina a lippy kiss; the animals assume funny bedtime positions, especially Ernest who "sleeps like a log," which indeed he resembles.

Some of the verbal humor, however, seems condescending to children, relying on inappropriate adult wit: "One marble means 'Come!'; two marbles means 'Come with your car!'; three marbles means 'Hurry up with your car!'" Or again, "It's better never to mention a lady's age." Indeed, Laurent seems to be an outsider rather than a participant in this story, inventing activities for characters he doesn't know as well as Babar or care about as much as Bonhomme.

The next two stories are more verbally direct and visually interesting, but as "a compromise between the Babars and myself," even they are not yet fair measures of Laurent's originality and artistry. He believes these stories are "too close to Babar but not as good—only OK."

Serafina's Lucky Find (1962) is "an old boat abandoned on the river bank . . . full of holes." The adventure, this time less wordy and in past tense, is how the five friends work to make the boat waterworthy and yet still have time for horseplay. They get caught in the rain, locked in a house, dumped into the water, and fed hot chocolate by indulgent Grandmother Giraffe. They play pranks on one another, call names ("Imbeciles!", "old grouch"), argue, and then, just as easily come to each other's aid. Laurent, whose own children were now of school age, again shows childhood relationships with more candor than his father. Except for their occasional lovable pranks, Jean's fictional children were models of decorum.

Patrick, who "detested water" is more mischievous than in *Serafina;* he teases Beryl and plagues Hugo with his antics. Hugo, who masterminds the repair project, is still capable and task-oriented, annoyed when his lighthearted friends won't work but quick to the rescue when the boat capsizes. Solid Ernest plays a vital role and even skittish Serafina helps a little, though, as usual, she doesn't think ahead.

The pictures have more vitality than those in *Serafina* because strong blue has been added and line is more vigorous. Blue skies, water, and house contrast cleanly with two shades of green and the oranges. Facial expressions are more telling, and action, such as the rain, Patrick's mischief, and the boat capsizing, has intensity. Humor abounds: Patrick in rubber boots and umbrella, Ernest with feet through the boat, the animals' Greek chorus, and Serafina mufflered against a cough.

Laurent has filled this tale with bits of childish business that could well amuse young readers; he seems more comfortable with tone, not quite so "above" his story as in *Serafina*. But there is still not much to pore over and little to remember beyond the lighthearted activities.

In *Captain Serafina* (1963) the summer is over, and Serafina is ready to go home. With her four friends, "instead of taking the train" she travels in her *Lucky Find* sailboat, now named *Dragonfly*. The watery odyssey, told again in past tense, has more excitement than the other two Serafinas, but the familiar characters are consistently feisty and a possible theme for the trilogy emerges.

Three bicker over who will be captain: "It's my boat, so I will be captain" declares Serafina, letting Hugo the kangaroo be pilot and Ernest the crocodile accompany the baggage in a dinghy; Patrick the rabbit has a tantrum, which prompts long-suffering Hugo to call him "idiot." In the fracas, the boat runs aground and has a rough passage before it reaches the sea, where Beryl the frog is scalded by the salt water. Serafina chokes on a bone because "as usual she ate too fast"; no sooner has she regained composure than a storm threatens the little craft and eventually casts Ernest adrift. Luckily, he is saved and, "crying with weariness," joins his friends who ingeniously complete the homeward journey, despite a broken mast. These mishaps make for a lively plot, though none carries as much emotional intensity as when Babar feels angry, frightened, sad, or stranded, and the reader is only mildly engaged in the action.

There are some calm interludes, too: the voyage begins so peacefully that Serafina breaks into song; the day at the beach gives a variety of pleasures; and the reunions are filled with hugs and kisses of real affection, though again not as emotionally charged as when Babar gives hugs and kisses.

Illustrations in flat blues, greens, and oranges are not quite as vivid as those in *Lucky Find;* again the major strength of the line drawings is movement rather than detail. Idyllic calm fills the first double spread as the boat starts up the winding river; in contrast, the storm scene conveys high wind velocity, though the waves are not convincing. And when Ernest finds himself washed up onto shore, the picture—the best in the book—minimally but powerfully shows his lonely weariness.

The Serafina books are bridges between Laurent's first six Babars and his later work. They lack the substance and intriguing fantasy of the elephant books and the free yet purposeful whimsicality of *A tue-tête* and, later, *Bonhomme* and *The One Pig with Horns.* A professional transition, however, the trilogy gave him a creative way of temporarily containing Babar while trying out his own style and insights into the nature of "un-utopian" children.

Anatole and His Donkey

Rather than animals, Laurent chooses a human protagonist in this story dedicated to Antoine his son. He uses to charming and eloquent effect a cumulative folktale plot pattern that is new to his work. Although Random House would be Babar's sole American publisher, for his non-Babar books Laurent tried different U.S. houses. Michael de Capua, editor for *Anatole and His Donkey* (1963), moved shortly afterwards to Pantheon, where Laurent "followed" him for his later non-Babar stories, thus accounting for the single volume with Macmillan and the book's atypical 10-by-7-inch size.

Anatole is a countryman with flair—top hat to cover sparse hair, bright orange suit, and a moustache that is the barometer of his emotions. With nicely cadenced prose, he sets off happily one morning to find "a sweet and gentle donkey. . . . To draw the little cart, to take the vegetables to market. To keep him company."[2] The Cattle Merchant has no donkey but sells Mr. Anatole first an ox, then a sheep, then a goat, all excellent purchases but unfortunately not the donkey he yearns for. This trio, together with a frog he finds, tries to distract their kind master by imitating the hee-haw he craves. But, though Anatole "smiled at them sadly," his sighing—and his progressively droopier moustache— is more than they and a barn owl can bear. At this point the cumulative pattern reaches its peak.

Then, in reverse order, the faithful animals leave to seek the donkey that will bring happiness back to Anatole's face. But as they go one by one, he realizes how much his donkey obsession has clouded his need and affection for them. When the ox is finally ready to set off, "Anatole lost heart. 'Oh, ox, don't go. You won't find my donkey, and I'll be all alone.'" Even the ox's confident "I'll bring you back a donkey" does not assure Anatole, who "was alone now, more alone than before. His moustache drooped on each side of his mouth" and, despairing, he hides his head in his hands.

But, just at the story's nadir, "all of a sudden . . . he was awakened by a hee-haw!" of the longed-for donkey with the "gray velvet nose" that his friends had returned with. A kiss, a hug, and a joyous donkey ride with Anatole's moustache flying bring the story to its happily-ever-after, full-circle ending.

Illustrations are in the style of *A tue-tête*, though the satire is much gentler, and they have touches of orange. Facial expressions and body attitudes convey emotion with few but careful lines: not only does Anatole's moustache droop but his whole body sags as he saddens. There is little background to distract from characters and plot, allowing uncluttered white space to intensify loneliness and the passage of time.

In spite of its past tense, the text has vitality and a poetic simplicity, achieved by frequent use of short, parallel structures— "You're right, I'll take the ox" and "You're right, I'll take the sheep"—and folktale conventions like action in threes and the plot pattern itself. Never wordy, the directness of Laurent's language—and Richard Howard's graceful translation—complements the clean candor of the pictures to create an emotionally satisfying whole.

Here is a gentle fable—Laurent never would be moralistic—about the need for and joys of friendship. Anatole is a sort of working-class Everyman, universal in his search for affection; but the animals are like people, too, as the donkey's response to his new master shows with touching clarity. The is the first of Laurent's non-Babar stories that reveals his distinctive vision, original style, and storytelling ability. Justifiably, it is one of his favorites.

The Lesson Books

After meeting Robert Bernstein of Random House in Paris in 1962, Laurent contracted for three Babar books that bypassed Hachette. This American collaboration soon proved so congenial that Random House became Laurent's primary publisher, an arrangement that cannot have pleased Hachette after its 30-year corner on first-edition Babars. But Laurent liked the artistic freedom he had with the American firm and flourished with the liaison. He continued, however, to write in French, approving translations done by various Random House editors, often unnamed.

For the Lesson Books, which were identical except for their non-English vocabulary, the uncredited French was the work of Walter Retan and the "Spanish words [were] by Roberto Eyzaguirre." Hachette, which still had all international rights to Babar and published most of Laurent's subsequent books a year or two after the American editions, offered the lesson books in English, German, Italian, Portuguese, and Spanish editions in the late 1960s;[3] Random House, however, reprinted none of these.

With the new professional leaf came a change in picture technique. Using the method of Jean's first two books, Laurent submitted for reproduction the finished pictures, with color and black line on a single sheet, instead of line drawings that had to be colored from proofs. The less cumbersome process allowed for more spontaneity and suited Laurent's artistic needs for the next 20 years. At Random House first-edition major narratives were approximately 9 by 13 inches, only 1½ inches smaller than Hachette's old "Big Babars"; subsequent mainstream stories (except *Babar and the Ghost*, 1981) would retain these larger-than-usual dimensions, although reprint sizes would vary.

The publisher's introduction to both *Babar's French Lessons* and *Babar's Spanish Lessons* says, "Babar knows what boys and girls like, and so he has chosen to instruct them in those words and phrases that they are most likely to use from day to day." Perhaps. But the vocabulary, mostly nouns and verbs set in an occasional present-tense sentence, is primarily the daily language of *Babar's* world: *ma couronne, mi corona* (my crown); *des croissants, medias lunas* (crescents); *mon bateau a voile, mi barco de vela* (my sailboat); *je conduis, manejo* (I drive); *j'allume ma pipe, enciendo mi pipa* (I light my pipe), and so forth. In 14 scenes of regular activities for the Babar family—eating, going to school, walking in the garden, playing soccer, riding bicycles, celebrating a birthday, etc.—the serene life-style of the elephants is verbally and visually confirmed. Some scenes remind readers of other books: Babar's bedroom admission "sometimes I have nightmares" of *Babar the King;* the walk in the rain of *P* in *A.B.C. of Babar;* and the blue Citroën named Josephine of the rare time that Laurent drew real cars in *Babar and the Professor.*

In this book of language lessons, with English words in heavy black type and French or Spanish equivalents in blue, there are also Babar's unmistakable courtesy lessons, conveyed in pictures and words: how to take a proper shower, eat a balanced breakfast ("breakfast is very important, isn't it?"), write neatly ("Be careful not to make ink spots"), avoid greediness ("do not eat too large a piece"), and puddles ("do you like to jump into them? That's not very nice"), and so forth.

The youngsters show some new traits: Arthur, as well as Pom, is greedy; Alexander cries, a behavior that is usually Flora's. But their birthday requests reassure readers that Pom is still aggressively manly, Flora feminine, artistic, and a little timid, and Alex-

98   JEAN AND LAURENT DE BRUNHOFF

ander adventurous. The first-person text is conversational, with Babar addressing an English-speaking American audience who learn a little French in one book, a little Spanish in the other. Although Laurent disputes that the Babars are particularly Gallic, the details he illustrates confirm their Frenchness: no milk, cereal, or orange juice on the breakfast table, soccer but not baseball, French bread in the knapsack, a French-style cake and car, and a map of France for the geography lesson; Babar the Frenchman has, after all, not yet internationalized his imagery by visiting America or even more exotic places.

These illustrated elephant vignettes may not be as detailed or informative as those in Jean's *A.B.C. of Babar,* but there are charming moments: Babar briskly rubbing his stomach in the shower; Babar holding a book with his trunk alone, thus freeing his "hands" to smoke one of two fine pipes; and Arthur waterskiing adeptly. Not surprisingly, Babar has acquired a new bedroom since *Babar the King,* an ornate Louis XIV suite, complete with bedside decanter and wine glass, telephone, and crown hook. And though he wears his customary green suit, bow tie, and crown, he occasionally needs spectacles, as the title page illustration suggests.

In *Babar's Lessons,* unencumbered by story, Laurent is free to illustrate what he chooses without the demands of narrative continuity. These books, the same except for their language, look ahead to future nonnarrative works, particularly activity books and calendars, in which Laurent's skills as painter flourish.

Bonhomme

Shortly after Laurent de Brunhoff made the move that changed his life in 1985, he sketched in sure black paint a large, new portrait of Bonhomme for his small, new studio in Middletown. There is a freedom, a puckish joie de vivre about that figure that announces itself as the artist's truest persona, even after 20 years. Indeed, de Brunhoff has a "special feeling" about Bonhomme, his most original creation, and he pours it generously into this story

dedicated to his daughter Anne.[4] A second Bonhomme book, typical of Laurent's quite different style a decade later, unfortunately
lacks this story's spontaneous freshness and wit.

Emilie is a little girl, lonely perhaps, who focuses her telescope
on "a funny little man . . . [with] a thorn growing out of the back
of his head." He sits under a distant tree on a red mountain;

Emille visits Bonhomme. From *Bonhomme* by Laurent de Brunhoff. Copyright
1965 by Random House, Inc. Reprinted by permission of Pantheon Books, a
division of Random House, Inc.

"sometimes Emilie sees him walking, but most of the time he stays beside the tree, as if he were thinking." He so intrigues her with his self-contained stillness that she climbs the red-pink rocks where she discovers that he is "round as he can be," "gentle and shy," excitable, funny, gallant—an altogether *bonhomme* and ideal friend.

Worried by Emilie's absence, however, her parents ask help from local authorities, who shut the strange little Bonhomme up in the zoo. His self-defining head spike, a threat to everyone but Emilie, wilts under the ignominy and penned-up loneliness—and only by Emilie's intervention is he freed, with a neutralizing "cork on the end of his spike."

Emilie's parents are kind, and Bonhomme enjoys the amenities of their home—"good things to eat," the bathroom mirror, Papa's cigars, which "he smokes two at a time," and special treatment when he sleeps. But when Emilie leaves for school, Bonhomme "gets bored"—lonely, trapped, out of his element—and, discarding the alien cork "behind the door," quietly returns to his home under the mountain tree.

At first Emilie stares bleakly out of her window when "Bonhomme does not come back." But inaction and self-pity are no answer. And so, in the spirit of Babarian determination, "ever since that day, Emilie often goes walking on the mountain. And when she comes back she says, with a funny little face, 'I saw Bonhomme today.'"

The text is elegantly simple, not a word too much, and it is beautifully integrated with the minimalist, strong-line pictures. Bonhomme is wispy, fey, naive, all of which Laurent conveys with remarkably free but precise line. Bonhomme racing after himself under the tree or mugging before the mirror are inspired bits of directed energy, and the town council caricatures are pungent. The tree on top of red mountains is splendidly isolated yet enticing as it perches left on the title and right on the closing page, nicely bracketing the whole book.

Bonhomme is not the instrument of moral message like Babar or didactic directive like Tomi Ungerer's quietly cautionary Moon

Man,[5] a favorite of Laurent's. Yet he is clearly an individual threatened by the need to conform, a sweet, rather egocentric dreamer who resists socialization just as children do. They will probably not give the sexual reading that Weber seems bent on (Weber, 130, 139, 185); fortunately, the story has meaning beyond a reductive fettered-phallus interpretation. Bonhomme's spike is more than an oddly placed penis, his confinement more than emasculation, and his returning home more than restlessness or the quest for male potency. Freedom is a spiritual need felt by both sexes, as it was by Bonhomme. Neither all-child nor all-adult, the inscrutable little misfit ultimately chooses freedom to be himself, a difficult choice children and artists must make, too.

Babar Comes to America

Following closely Laurent and Marie-Claude's monthlong trip to America in 1963, this 66-page book is a chronicle of Babar's "official visit," at the invitation of the president, to major U.S. points of interest.[6] The de Brunhoffs' trip was organized by Random House as preparation for the book and sponsored additionally by other U.S. companies. Not a dramatic narrative, *Babar Comes to America* (1965) is a kind of *Childe Harold's Pilgrimage*, a travelogue with reflections that reveal Babar's candid, if not always favorable, first impressions of the country Laurent would adopt.

From the title page, complete with anticipatory cowboy hat and three cameras, Babar is an eager tourist who leaves home, flies over Paris, and arrives at Dulles International Airport in Washington, D.C. Laurent draws a "very up-to-date terminal" and Babar gently satirizes the French image of Americans to the waiting press, "I am very happy to come to your great country, the country of Washington, of Mark Twain, of Danny Kaye."

But for the official duties, especially visiting all the monuments and museums, his enthusiasm wanes: "It is all very tiring." Upon seeing Smithsonian rocketry, a touch of Gallic jingoism prompts him to declare, "The first astronaut to set foot on the moon might well be an elephant!" Babar is, in fact, glad to pack away his crown and leave the capital for New York, "a city he has always wanted to see."

But his cheery excitement is short-lived: on Wall Street he "gets something in his eye"; bed and American breakfast at the Hilton are satisfactory, but the view is depressing; riding the elevator all the way down is *not* fun; the bus driver is rude; and on Fifth Avenue, "everyone seems to be in a hurry. No one looks at anyone else. . . . [T]he auto horns all honk at once," in distressing contrast to the friendly, leisurely main street portrayed in *Babar's Fair*. Eager to absorb everything but never before a gourmand, Babar overindulges in American food—a hamburger and a cheeseburger, "Coca-Cola, Pepsi-Cola, V-8, 7 Up, ginger ale . . . apple pie à la mode . . . a banana split and a chocolate soda"—and then, looking sick, buys antacid. Old landmarks disappear to make way for skyscrapers on streets that offer little beauty. There are some good moments in a Japanese restaurant, an antique shop, and a Greenwich Village jazz club; and Babar does enjoy the tranquility of Central Park where, fortunately, he does not get mugged. But he comes close to losing his identity again, and though Laurent denies any intentional irony or personal parallel ("I love New York!"), Babar's first two stops yield more pain than pleasure.

Only when he leaves to spend "a quiet weekend" at the suburban Scarsdale home of his friends "Bob and Helen" (Bob and Helen Bernstein were the de Brunhoffs' personal friends and hosts, too) does he come into his own, in spite of a supermarket traffic jam that makes him uncharacteristically clumsy. His best eastern moments are spent playing at home with the children or visiting Harvard's ivy-covered cloister where he is appreciated by his own cultivated kind.

The next stop is the Midwest and Detroit, where an automobile factory is fascinating until Babar loses his hat. He has only admiration for Chicago but comments wryly on the prowess and confidence of Lake Michigan fishermen: "no one beside the lake is eating fish! Everywhere are barbecue grills with skewered meat and spare ribs"; again, he is happiest playing father quietly with a child.

Perhaps because he is growing accustomed to American cities—
or perhaps because he meets his family there—Babar finds the
West, especially San Francisco, delightful: the Golden Gate, not
the first bridge Laurent has admired, is "as beautiful as a cathe-
dral"; the cable cars are fun to ride; the varied architecture and
Fisherman's Wharf catch Babar's artist's eye; even Alexander's
"naughty idea" and Pom's overloaded stomach cannot dim this
city's luster.

Babar had liked the cross-country Vistadome trip through the
Rockies, too; now the whole family enjoys a spectacular coastal
drive and cottage in Carmel; the boys love the ocean and beach
while Flora typically prefers the mission church garden. Babar
pilots a red convertible through sequoia-filled Yosemite and "blaz-
ing hot" Death Valley; he even conquers freeway traffic in Los
Angeles, which "is so big that one cannot tell where it begins or
where it ends." Of course, L.A. means a poolside Hollywood reception with the film crowd, a trip through urban blight—"forests of
telegraph poles and armies of oil-well pumps"—to Disneyland,
and a cowboy film at the drive-in movie.

On a helicopter side trip of their own, Babar and Arthur run
out of gas over the Arizona desert; eventually they make it to the
Grand Canyon, which Arthur, like Laurent, is not taken with, and
a powwow with local Indians. In Texas they buy cowboy clothes
and see a prize Black Angus bull; in New Orleans they love the
French Quarter balconies but especially, the "fried chicken and
pecan pie."

Finally the peripatetic family is reunited in the East to climax
their experiences with that typically American phenomenon, a
fall football game; the Harvard-Yale teams even "play with Arthur a few minutes, just for fun." A parting taste of upscale Amer-
icana before the Babars return home on an ocean liner is the
comfortable Thanksgiving turkey-and-trimmings dinner with
Bob and Helen. Then, almost abruptly, Céleste has a last-minute
shopping spree, porters tote luggage, and the elephant family,
"sad about leaving," waves farewell, carrying with them "the
memories of their wonderful trip to America."

With a few exceptions, the de Brunhoffs saw what Babar saw.

Their broad-swath America is a stylized but fairly recognizable rendering of major tourist attractions, distinctive cityscapes, and authentic suburban or rural environments. Laurent carefully shows the ethnic diversity of U.S. cities, drawing African Americans, Asian Americans, and native Americans with more racial sensitivity and authenticity than in the past. Unfortunately, he implies an inaccurate white exclusivity in suburbs and elite universities, and he seems blind to Hispanics in California.

Acknowledging the trip's sponsors—Pan American, Hilton Hotels, and American Airlines (though not Coca-Cola, V-8, Del Monte, or Kellogg)—Laurent celebrates American products by name and prominent people by parody, creating a jazz pianist, Theodorus Priest, and a Hollywood director, Urchin Walls. Some of the bright, cartoonlike illustrations are fairly detailed and have funny moments: Babar meeting some squirrels, building a sand castle, wearing sunglasses, balancing a cable car, and smoking a cigar; a Louis Armstrong look-alike trumpeter is as wrapped up in his work as the Lake Michigan fishermen, Carmel surfers, filmland sycophants and luggage-laden porters. Laurent delights in gently mocking American archetypes, as he had French ones in *A tue-tête,* and humorously captures the 1960s "look" right down to Jackie Kennedy pillbox hats.

The thoughtful comments of Robert Phelps fault de Brunhoff for drawing a frantic, nonreflective America, crass in its collective taste, "a superficial half-truth" apparently without libraries, art museums, symphony orchestras, or subtlety.[7] Considering that the visit was book-specific, the time limited, the itinerary deliberately planned—and that it was only his second trip to America—Laurent could hardly represent the country in all its richness. Instead he chose, perhaps not always wisely or according to his own tastes, images that invoke at least some of its geographical and cultural variety. That is was a "pretty upper middle-class tour"[8] (except for libraries, art museums, and symphonies) cannot be denied, but then neither Laurent de Brunhoff nor Babar ever protest their bourgeois roots.

"Realism is riskier than fantasy," says the man who would rather draw roadsters from childhood memories than actual automobiles. Laurent enjoyed the change this book afforded but would not do another Baedeker, even of the country he now knows better and could portray more completely. For Babar, the egalitarian elephant with a strong French accent, the trip through America was illuminating and ultimately wonderful. But always a family-centered utopian, he resists going native and instead goes home where his identity is undisputed.

Babar Loses His Crown

Readers who remember what happened when Babar lost his crown in *The Travels of Babar* might well be prepared for a tense adventure. However, this Beginner Book (part of the same series as Dr. Seuss's ground-breaking *Cat in the Hat*), with its limited vocabulary and simple cartoon illustrations, is reduced in excitement as well as size, so that Babar's search for his crown becomes only a mildly hectic trip through Paris. Except for Jean's *A.B.C. of Babar*, this is the first Babar designed expressly for the 7-by-9-inch format that eventually—and unfortunately—becomes one standard Babar size.

But why did Babar have to shrink this much? After 16 books that had perpetuated the elephants' world in large-scale grandeur, the small, oversimplified pictures and story diminish the elephant king's stature and minimize his world. Easy books like this have proliferated in America and abroad because children can read them alone; unfortunately, they usually do, since adults find little that lures them to share the skimpy pages. Economical, utilitarian, and profitable though they may be, small-size Babar narratives are for the most part artistically inferior to the splendid big books and far from springboards for the imagination.

In *Babar Loses His Crown* (1967) the Babars, not long back from America, take a train from Célesteville to Paris; at their hotel, Babar tells a porter, "Be careful with that little red bag. My crown is in it."[9] But alas, bags have gotten switched at the station and Céleste unpacks, "A flute! Babar! This is not your bag!" (10). His dismay, however—"My crown is gone!" (11)—lacks the angry helplessness he showed in *The Travels of Babar*. And the subsequent search for the man with Babar's red bag seems motivated less by Babar's urgency to recapture his identity than by Paris landmarks: the Ritz Hotel on place Vendôme, the Eiffel Tower overlooking prominent Right Bank sites like Palais de Chaillot and the Etoile; Seine boats and banks; the Tuileries; a typical outdoor café and market; place de la Concorde and arch de Triomphe; the Métro above and below ground; and the Opéra outside and in. Though drawn without much detail, these backgrounds dominate the story and minimize suspense about "Who has the crown and why?" The final double spread is interesting, not as denouement but as a reprise of Jean's theater scene in *Babar the King*, this time with *Dido and Aeneas* instead of Corneille and a human rather than elephant audience.

Characters act predictably, except for Babar, who shows uncharacteristic petulant vanity: "All those people will see me—ME, the king—without a crown! I just can't go in there!" (57). Perhaps some of the anxiety he felt in New York still lingers. In *The Travels of Babar*, however, when he was in real danger, he kept his dignity; here, where he is merely inconvenienced, he acts pettish.

Laurent has concentrated again on setting, his strong point in previous books; the small format, however, reduces the importance of his tribute to Paris, which pales beside large-scaled Célesteville in *Babar's Fair*, sprawling Los Angeles in *Babar Comes to America*—or Ludwig Bemelmans's big-page Paris in the Madeline books. Pictures are heavier in line and color than previously, making even action scenes, like the chaos in the marketplace, seem stolid. Happily, they do retain some de Brunhoff humor: rotund elephants "hide" behind slim trees, and *parisiennes* are unerringly, if sometimes ludicrously, stylish.

Language limitations, on the other hand, are handled fairly well, the minimal text being a collaboration between Laurent and Random House editors. Though sentences are short, they are well cadenced and nicely balanced: Babar says, "I can wear a crown. But I can't wear a flute," whereupon the accidental thief replies, "I can play a flute. But I can't wear a crown" (*Crown*, 61). At the end, "the crown is on the head of the King. . . . and the flute is under the Mustache-man's mustache" (*Crown,* 62, 63). The illustrations retain their original French, with *bateau mouche* (an actual Seine River passenger boat), *correspondance* (transfer), *sortie* (exit), and *restaurant* subtly defying the limits imposed on English vocabulary.

Picture stories for beginning readers are a laudable concept; some are artistic as well as popular. But Babar is too substantial to be confined to such limiting visual and verbal formats. In trying to fit Babar into its Seussian mold, Random House has done a disservice to the originality of both Seuss and de Brunhoff. Alas, Babar will be reduced in small books of varying size for years to come.

The Pop-up Books

Disappointing Babar lovers even more are these pop-up stories— *Babar's Games* (1968) and *Babar's Moon Trip* (1969)—that, though they bear Laurent de Brunhoff's name, have neither his text nor his illustrations. Instead, Japanese technicians who devised the fold-outs did both story and pictures, working from very minimal sketches and ideas by Laurent. Clearly an attempt to capitalize on timely world events—the 1968 Olympics and the 1969 moon walk—these stiffly wordy books are generally more mechanical than interesting, more commercial than artistic. Out of print now but still included in Babar bibliographies, these two volumes are important only as early evidence of Laurent's relinquishing artistic control over what publishers considered potentially lucrative Babar "merchandise." As such, they forecast Babar films, books, and other enterprises that imply—but in fact are not—de Brunhoff work.

"Little Babar" Sets

In yet another less-than-lustrous venture, Laurent's format experiments continue with the publication of three boxed sets of small 5-by-4-inch hardbound books—*Babar's Trunk, Babar's Other Trunk, Babar's Bookmobile*—four to a set, making a total of twelve Random House "Little Babars."[10] Hachette had published the French originals in 1966, 1969, and 1970, in a different format (similar to the 1952 episodes from Jean's stories); shortly after, Methuen published its own "Little Babar" series.

These 12-page books, though appealing to child-size hands and publishers' gift lists, are mere shadows of full-length Babar stories. Laurent now agrees that they "are not at all as interesting" because "they were made for Hachette with my design and rough drawings, the final art done by the publisher," whose formulized line and color make even skiing and swimming seem static and boxed in. The simple text, also done in editorial collaboration with the publisher, though not technically an "easy reader," is scaled well enough to the small size; but with so little picture artistry, the few words beg for European script rather than sharp-edged American printing.

Babar's Trunk (1969) centers on family activity, not, as the title suggests, on Babar alone; some episodes have moments of excitement like getting lost, stung, soaked, or scolded; others just meander through favorite pastimes like gardening, eating, driving, scuba-diving—familiar work and play that is explored better in the bigger books. Rather flatly, appropriate behavior is reinforced, and personalities and family relationships are consistent.

Babar's Other Trunk (1971) shows Babar using skills and talents introduced in earlier books, parlaying his "setting-up exercises" (*The Story of Babar*, 19) into winning a marathon; his support of the arts (*Babar the King*) into personal painting; and his tenting abilities (*The Travels of Babar*) into an eventful family camping trip, while Céleste and the Old Lady hone nursing skills first practiced in *Babar and His Children*. *Babar's Bookmobile* (1974) looks back on other stories, too: Babar once again rescues Arthur; tries and fails to bake one of the spectacular sweets he adores; puts up his own Christmas tree with some difficulty; and repairs a violin so that the family concert can continue.

But in all of these books the palette is too confined, with no room for grand enlargements of scene, saga, or imagination. The skimpy, mechanically drawn stories may please very young readers and sell well, but they have little artistic merit and are poor showcases for Babar—and de Brunhoff.

Babar's Birthday Surprise

Nearly 10 years elapsed between *Babar's Castle* and *Babar's Birthday Surprise* (1970), which became Laurent's seventh mainstream Babar narrative only by a fortunate default.[11] It had been planned as another Beginner Book, with a slight story and small pictures. When that format proved impossible, Laurent had to expand the idea and illustrations, no easy task for a painter who found plotting difficult and the rut of unchallenging books becoming nearly habitual. But the American trip was still in his mind, and the image of Babar on a mountain fueled development of a full-length story that stemmed for a while the powerful tide of little books.

Certainly Queen Céleste would not have commissioned Podular to "carve a giant statue of King Babar right in the side of the mountain" if Laurent de Brunhoff had not been awed by Mount Rushmore. How Céleste's huge birthday gift is executed and kept a secret from the freewheeling Babar is the main plot of the story, told in rather flat prose but bold, colorful pictures.

Babar's Birthday Surprise maintains the conventions of earlier Babars, beginning and ending at home and offering advice on proper behavior throughout. The familiar extended family does its usual activities: walking among friends in the lush gardens; bicycling and driving red cars or interesting trucks; having an ample picnic with both soda and *vin ordinaire;* and planning a celebration complete with impressive birthday cake and musical ensemble. Old friends appear, too: Cornelius, Dr. Capoulosse, Madame Cesarine, Poutifour the gardener, the marabou messengers from *The Story of Babar* and *Babar's Picnic*. Daily family activity provides the action as Babar's favorite pipe gets lost and then broken when Flora accidentally steps on it; so nearly does Arthur's trunk when the children "jump wildly about on the scaffolding" and it collapses. Character is consistent, with teenage Arthur and Zephir alternating between mischievous and responsible behavior; the triplets are typically lively, a little quarrelsome, but not really individuated, though Flora does cry in one picture. Céleste the planner is more competent than in most of Laurent's stories, an attempt, perhaps, to bring her in line with Laurent's own feminist thinking; Babar is genial but seems a little dim not to suspect the goings-on.

With action that is hardly gripping, characters that are almost too familiar, and words that do little more than explain the pictures, the reader must focus on a few notable illustrations as the rewards of this story. Here Laurent the painter is strong. In the double-spread panorama of ever-expanding Célesteville, the view from "Mount Babar-Rushmore" shows that the original thatched native huts and palace are now surrounded by homes of an unusual style—and skyscrapers! The palm-lined riverbanks are joined by a new bridge, different from the elephant span that led to Babar's fair. Even Babar on a bike, dangerously close to discovering the sculpture, does not distract from the tableau of Célesteville's progress. In fact, its sudden evolution—not shown, after all, since *Babar and the Professor* 15 years earlier—almost begs for a map and chronology to systematize when and how it all came about.

Another pleasure worth waiting for is the unveiling. "The trumpets sound the fanfare. At this signal all the birds covering the mountain fly up at the same time. The air is filled with the loud fluttering of wings. Babar is stupefied. . . . 'What an enormous surprise!'" Indeed, the double spread of "millions of birds" whirling away from the giant face they have been hiding is a grand visual climax that far surpasses the verbal description. A wing-filled blue sky above and cheering Célestevillians below frame the pink mountain figure; readers can almost hear the trumpeters and feel the fanning of birds in flight as they wheel in outward circles from the statue. In this kinetic painting, one of his best, Laurent makes music from motion to stunning effect.

Except for the verbal wit of "Oh! How handsome Papa is as a mountain!" and the seriocomic theme of immortalizing Babar in craggy stone, Laurent's humor comes through mainly in his pictures: the dancing elephant sculpture that looks surprisingly graceful despite its bulk; Podular intensely wielding the pneumatic drill; Poutifour watering flowers and Cornelius conducting a sextet, each with his inexhaustible trunk; Babar puffing his glued-together pipe and Arthur manfully managing his bandaged proboscis.

Beyond the fact that it signaled Laurent's welcome return to mainstream Babar narrative, perhaps the most singular distinction of this story is that Jean could not have done it; he never visited America and so did not feel the impact of the presidential mountain. Only Laurent could bring Mount Rushmore to Célesteville and introduce this particular imagery naturally into Babar's world. Here he reaches beyond territory that Jean created—for imaginative though they were, Arab and native villages, the fair, Mammoth's cave, Castle Bonnetrompe, and even Bird Island were all close to the elephant utopia. With *Babar's Birthday Surprise*, de Brunhoff *fils* makes a significant transition from Laurent as Jean to Laurent as himself. The uneasy decade of eschewing father-faithfulness had ended. With this 1970 return to Babar on his own terms, Laurent showed a promising new vitality.

Gregory and the Lady Turtle in the Valley of the Music Trees

Yet another unfamiliar Laurent de Brunhoff surfaces in this unusual book: "I love to write. I wanted to write a long story." Thus motivated, Laurent has written, not a variant of the hare and tortoise fable, but a rambling tale about the relationship between a rabbit who likes machines and adventure and a turtle who prefers to eat lettuce and watch television. There are many words and few pictures. But even in a sensitive translation like Richard Howard's (1971), it is not surprising that American children have little interest in this story full of adult wit yet little dramatic point.[12]

Gregory, a decidedly jumpy rabbit, is determined that he and his lady friend will see the Valley of the Music Trees in his new, James Bond–like "red egg-shaped vehicle." Lady is reluctant and Gregory isn't quite sure where it is, but he heeds the advice of an eagle, "the only one who knows," and bores through a mountain. On the other side the pair meets Lonely Horse who inexplicably has a television set, whereupon Lady enthuses, "I adore watching TV!" But Gregory lets nothing get in the way of his mission and finally the trio reaches the Music Trees that have "musical instruments . . . hanging" from their branches—"violins, cellos, flutes, clarinets and bassoons." An orchestra of llamas, antelopes, and sheep plays intensely; "Gregory's ears quiver with pleasure, and the turtle sways her head from left to right." Suddenly the musicians stop, hang up their instruments—and go to sleep.

Next morning, Lonely Horse wakes everyone urgently with his collar of bells, for "you never wake up again, if you stay under the Music Trees after sunrise." Lady Turtle is still curled peacefully under her shell, dreaming of lettuce, but they manage to wake her with special water so that she is alert enough to watch television. After this comes a rainstorm, a flood, and a plague of snails that make Lady Turtle want even more to go home.

Because the rain has washed away even the musical evenings, Lady is more bored than usual. To get her mind off television and lettuce, Gregory does daredevil tricks with his red machine, boring swiss-cheese holes into the mountains. His antics end in the worse way possible—he crashes into the television set and arouses the displeasure of the eagle who agrees to find another set just to save his mountains from the hazardous rabbit. Eventually—and without much logic—the musicales begin again, Gregory saves the animals from eternal sleep, the new television arrives, the red car gets fixed, and Lady Turtle finally gets home to her own lettuce.

The relationship between Gregory and Lady has satirical undertones that probably amuse Laurent and other adults more than children: she is the quintessential tolerant female, coping with the whims of an action-oriented, not-too-perceptive mate. Similarly, Greg is Everymale, putting up with Lady's lack of pioneering spirit and her persistent badgering to go home. Even their names for each other—"Turtledove," "my old nutshell," "Greg"—satirize adult terms of endearment. Other characters seem beside the point. Why is he called Lonely Horse—because he watches too much television? Because he is the solitary one responsible for waking the sleepers? What purpose do crow, owl, and the animal musicians really have in the story?

Language flows smoothly enough, and sometimes Richard Howard's translation is quite lovely: "Night comes down from the mountains," and "The umbrellas are ripe, soon it will rain." Dialogue is not stilted, though sometimes the point of view is inconsistent, as when Lady says to no one in particular, "This rabbit is crazy, utterly crazy." But the words have nowhere to go, no coherent dramatic point.

The best part of the book is the pictures, too few, but welcome oases of fast-paced delight. As always, Laurent excels at black-line movement: the first dash across the valley with hare and turtle on the galloping horse's back; the concert; the rainstorm; the animals' farewell as the visitors leave. Reds and pinks enliven the clean black lines to vivid or muted effect.

This leisurely venture into storytelling was published subsequently by L'Ecole des Loisirs in a collection that French children love. But the serendipitous plot and unsympathetic characters miss the expectations of American readers, who eagerly accepted the Frenchness of Babar and Bonhomme.

After 10 years' experimentation with form and substance, Laurent de Brunhoff's balance sheet showed minuses and pluses. Perhaps justifiably, he had succumbed to pressures for commercially profitable but artistically unrewarding Babar ventures, principally less-than-distinguished books and a plethora of by-products. On the other hand, he had developed characters in a style uniquely his own and found a way to give his father's elephant king his own Laurent signature.

6

The Artistic Resolution of Babar's Legacy
Laurent de Brunhoff's Stories since 1972

While still testing different ideas and formats during these two productive decades, Laurent began to integrate his independent impulses with his Babar mission. He introduced yet more non-Jean elements, not all of them equally felicitous to Babar purists, and wrote another non-Babar book. He celebrated the elephant king's fiftieth birthday and developed further the lighter, more painterly style of illustration. Most important, he turned his—and Babar's—personal life around and achieved an artistic confidence and serenity that was close to, if different from, his father's.

Babar Visits Another Planet

In *Babar Visits Another Planet* (1972), another story his father could not have done, Laurent has let his considerable imagination run free with ingenious settings, strange new characters, suspense, and an unsettling outcome.[1] Misjudged by some critics, it is one of Laurent's most original but disquieting Babar stories.[2]

The elephant king and his family are having an idyllic picnic lunch when Arthur looks up and exclaims, "Look, a rocket . . . [I]t's going to land!" Not only does it land rudely near the Babars with a windy "WHIRR" but "sucks them right into the cabin . . .

[and] carries them off into space" all in the first two pages! "Céleste is frantic" and even Babar is worried and not a little annoyed at their intergalactic imprisonment. But the children love the pilotless journey that provides a good view of the stars, "some biscuits held out to them by an automatic arm," and even soothing music.

"After many days," through blue skies, past the moon and Mars, the rocket lands on an uncharted red planet with a sticky surface that captures one of Babar's shoes. Luckily, its odd inhabitants who "look like elephants, but yet they're not elephants," welcome the earth folks "in a most friendly manner," and transport them over the caramel surface in pink "skimmercraft" and transparent "flying eggs." The city-in-the-sky, with its white, pueblolike houses on different platforms and levels, is suspended stunningly from enormous red balloons, reminiscent of William Pène du Bois's *Twenty-one Balloons*.[3] Even cautious Céleste "forgets to be dizzy" as the family is initiated into the wondrous, if frustrating, oddities of space language and customs.

At the home of their hosts and royal counterparts, Pointed Hat and Blue Mushroom, the Babars find unexpected luxury, even "a swimming pool in the living room," and unstinting hospitality; the pool is even "emptied and filled with pillows" so that bulky Babar and Céleste, too large for the family's built-in beds, can have a comfortable place to sleep. Breakfast, "cakes and soft drinks," is served from an automatic fountain, pleasing everyone but Babar, who prefers more genteel dining; he is again disappointed at the shoe store, deciding for the sake of elegance, "to take off his remaining shoe" when he can't be fit. In fact, though his behavior is gentlemanly in the face of all these inconveniences, Babar has not been comfortable since he left home.

The jousting tournament of flying eggs gives Babar pleasure though—until Arthur's egg bounces too high, rips into a balloon with its parking hook, and "the air rushes out!" The platform tilts Titanic-like and everyone scrambles frantically to another level. Luckily no one is harmed and a flying repair crew replaces the damaged support almost at once.

But though "danger is over," the near disaster has disturbing consequences. "The natives . . . seem annoyed. They frown and complain bitterly." Babar and Pointed Hat know that Arthur, who also has suffered from the accident, had not purposely burst the balloon. But Pointed Hat fears for his guests' safety. "This might be dangerous for you. . . . It might be better for you to return to earth." Regretfully, he says farewell to the earthlings he was so eager to meet, and the family leaves as unceremoniously as they came. Babar "looks back pensively" as the rocket takes them up through blackness to Célesteville and home.

Back in Célesteville, the Old Lady, "still very upset, is crying. 'Why did they kidnap you so brutally?'" Babar gives a diplomatic answer, but the more troubling question, "Why did they turn on us?" is left unasked and unanswered. Future connections with the soft planet will apparently be up to the children who loved it: as her link to the floating city, Flora has the "little blue puppy," a benign creature who predicts the Wully-Wully; Arthur is youthfully sure that "we can telephone . . ." and hopes "that they will come to see us in Célesteville."

Laurent has invented another seriocomic world, but this one is untypical of the Babars—just as the unresolved *Q* conflicts in Jean's *A.B.C. of Babar* are an isolated occurrence. It *looks* funny, with pear-shaped air taxis that fit inhabitants' figures perfectly; playgroundlike living areas full of slides, ladders, and interesting niches; colorful eating and shopping; airy architecture suspended by balloons in innocent blue skies. But it really isn't funny, for the surface is dangerous, balloons break, communication is unreliable, and people eventually *do* "appear menacing." From the beginning, Babar is unable to adapt to the planet his children love; the anxiety he showed but worked through in *Babar Comes to America* and *Babar Loses His Crown* is never resolved, for he is expelled before he can adjust. Back home in Célesteville, he is once again in control and apparently happy, but his resilience is gone, and he seems older.

It is possible that Laurent got so caught up in fantasy engineering that he couldn't end the story satisfactorily in 32 pages; he admits that the residents' hostility is too sudden and the ending ambiguously abrupt. He did not consciously contrast blue skies on the outward journey with black on the Babars' ignominious return, yet the weight of colors is hard to ignore. He may not have meant this story to have serious implications for Babar's character, but they are inescapable: the Babar of *The Travels of Babar* or *Babar's Fair* would have coped imaginatively with, not left, the crisis; the visitor to Bird Island or America would have reveled in the new, if strange, milieu. Whether intentionally or not, the elephant king is recognizable only by his physical appearance. Somehow, familiar, stalwart Babar has been lost, temporarily at least, in space.

Short Stories for Young Readers

Laurent's continuing interest in quality books for young readers, coupled with a fresh concern for the integrity of his own artwork, resulted in a series of "sidestream" rather than mainstream Babars, little 8-by-8-inch stories for preschoolers that augment and update the saga in interesting, if not always significant, ways. As a result, these books are generally superior to the earlier (and smaller) "Little Babar sets."[4]

In the first, *Meet Babar and His Family* (1973), the nervous space-traveler regains his sweet aplomb as the familiar family pursues seasonal activities in strong-colored, full-page pictures that hardly need the scant text.

One morning Babar opens his window excitedly onto a sunny view of yellow-green, pink-and-white fruit trees that "seem to have opened overnight." "It's spring!" The children see birds in nests, ducklings on the lake, and ride their bikes with abandon; they celebrate the season by visiting old friends for tea, an activity that is appropriate for any season. But when summer comes, living is outdoors almost exclusively: tending the garden, playing tennis, swimming and sailing, or "riding through the countryside" in an open car; summer also offers ice-cream cones from the street vendor, large parties on the palace lawn, concerts around the bandstand, and even walks in the rain. Nature is lushly green and blue and pink, and gardens are bountiful with fruits and flowers that seem to bloom endlessly.

With autumn come different rhythms—raking and walking in twilight leaves, going to school warmly dressed, playing soccer— in a world of rich oranges, russets, and browns. Finally, winter's chilly whites bring skating, mountain skiing, cotton-ball snow fights and ice sculptures, and the anticipation of Christmas, as the children look out at the wan winter evening, "hoping to catch a glimpse of Santa Claus."

Some pictures are outstanding for their color and mood: the spring orchard smiles with new life, and the lake in summer looks invitingly cool; burning leaves seem almost to perfume the autumn walk, and the dun-colored winter sky is textured with huge white snowflakes that become dun themselves against the whiter snow. Some scenes bring to mind other books, both Jean's and Laurent's, as the family does its daily rounds and personalities are confirmed. A larger format would have given the illustrations even more importance, but in this small size, they clearly dominate and are the raison d'être for the painter Laurent's most visually pleasing "pictureback."

In the second book in this series, *Babar Saves the Day* (1976), Babar proves how up to date he is by royally hosting a rock star, "Olala, the famous folk singer," and his band. Typical preteens by now, the children dog their idol's footsteps from airport to hotel to rehearsal. When Olala quarrels with his temperamental backup parrot, Kawak, the young Babars follow the bird everywhere. Finally his pique is spent, he is forgiven by Olala—"I am not angry any longer. Let's forget about our silly fight"—and the show goes on, complete with Kawak's "loud cou-acs during every chorus." When Céleste asks, "Do you *really* like that kind of music?" Babar bravely answers, "Of course, I do . . . but I don't think it needs so many cou-acs."

The minimal text, like *Meet Babar and His Family,* is short and uncomplicated. Some long words (hippopotamus, crocodile, amusement, interrupt, disappeared) and names (Célesteville, Cornelius, Boho, Crax) appear, making readers wonder why the gardener isn't named Poutifour and the mechanic Olur, just for old time's sake.

Even without the compelling attraction of large-size double spreads, a few pictures stand out: at the hotel haven, guests lounge and swim as a waiter brings liquid refreshment; Flora falls down and doesn't cry, braver since her encounter with Rataxes and Wully-Wully (part of a full-length book that had been published in 1975); Olala and Arthur chase Kawak though the dark subterranean Cave of the Mammoths, first visited in *Babar and the Professor;* Olala caresses his guitar under a classic portico anachronistically equipped with mikes and speakers while a motley audience "claps loudly." The humorous incongruity of it all is especially evident: Olala's chubby pinkness, the improbably graceful elephant statue, the so-1970s elephant hippie dressed in fringe, and, finally, the adolescents caught up in the rapture of Olala's rock sound.

If there is any theme to this trendy adventure, Babar the peacemaker articulates it when he assures rebellious Kawak that "Olala and the others need you very badly." Readers cannot help feeling sorry, however, that the elephant king, formerly a Mozart man, has been reduced to facilitator with dubious musical taste.

From the title page of *Babar Learns to Cook* (1978), readers would assume a feast of desserts, all concocted by Babar. Actually, Babar only watches and eats; it is the others—TV's Chef Truffles, the children, and Céleste—who whip up golden-brown stuffed mushrooms, sloppy green cucumber soup, velvety chocolate sauce, and Babar's favorite, strawberry soufflé.

This book is a lighthearted manual of what to do and what not to do in the kitchen. From crisp cordon bleu chef's hat to impeccable chopping and stirring technique, Chef Truffles shows why he is "the most famous chef in Célesteville"; Céleste capably demonstrates the art of the lofty soufflé; even Arthur "very seriously stirs a chocolate sauce" to great success. But the triplets create chaos with mixer, slicer, and blender that would outrage Chef Truffles, upsets even Céleste, and cautions young readers. Only after the food has been elegantly served and consumed does the chef regain composure and reward everyone with medals *and* hats, thanks to feminist Flora.

A few pictures are detailed: the palace kitchen is modernly stocked with tools and ingredients; the Babars still have many books in their blue-flowered livingroom but now own a large television as well; the amazing garden yields strawberries, carrots, and tomatoes at the same time. But in most cases, elephant shapes fill the square page, leaving little space for background detail.

This very slight story gives revealing glimpses of impish Alexander, adolescent Arthur, and now-assertive Flora. Little more than a sedentary gourmand, however, Babar the reassuringly authoritative father is sure to be missed by even little children.

With very few words and simple, undetailed pictures, *Babar the Magician* (1980), a smaller 6¼-inch-square, ring-bound book in the shape of Babar's crowned head, chronicles his achievements as a magician. He is just an apprentice, but, looking every inch the part, with blue moon-and-stars cape and two assistants, he succeeds in his amateur sleight of hand until he overdoes Zephir's hypnotic levitation! The stiff little monkey flies out of the palace, through the town, into the country and across the river; he disrupts a chess game, barely avoids a television antenna, ruins a painting, and gets bitten by a fish before he finally wakes, not remembering a thing. The only lasting memento of his trip is the fish, which Arthur catches neatly in a bowl.

For the first time since *Zephir's Holidays* the little monkey has his own story. But since he has no control over his behavior, it cannot even be said that the events either confirm or expand his character. Amateur magic is shown not to be one of Babar's talents, and he certainly is not in control of this situation. Other characters and settings are too small and/or brief to matter. The fast-moving plot may please very young readers, but pictures and words are not dramatic. All in all, the book, though an amusing change of pace for Laurent, is not a significant addition to the Babars, and Random House dropped the production-costly format soon after. Spanning seven years, these little stories kept pace with the times—and also with the subtle but disturbing change in Babar's traditionally authoritative character.

Bonhomme and the Huge Beast

In this second Bonhomme adventure, drawn in 1974 on the heels and in the mode of the colorfully fantastic *Babar Visits Another Planet,* the more painterly Laurent develops his enigmatic character further but not so distinctively as in the original, essentially black-and-white story.[5]

Emilie still visits her spiked friend's pink-mountain home but would like him to come to her house, too. At first reluctant, he finally agrees because "Bonhomme loves stories," and Emilie tells very good ones. Soon he spins his own, especially at bedtime, and to Emilie's Huge Frog tale he adds a Stone Horse yarn and another about a pink house. Surprisingly, their fantasies come to life (or dream): they ride a cloud to the amazing pink house, meet its huge but kind tenant Randolphe, "an enormous beast with tassels on its feelers and scales on its back," and explore the fascinating green pockets in his furry purple back. On finding a telephone in one, they call the Huge Frog and the Stone Horse, and soon everyone is making fantastic discoveries and playing vigorously.

Too vigorously though, for Stone Horse falls and "is broken to pieces!" Bonhomme is so sad that "his spike begins to curl," and as before when he was distressed, he "silently steals away." Faithful Emilie, on a well-repaired Stone Horse, searches for and finally finds Bonhomme. The friends have an affectionate reunion, and, tired of one fantasy, they dream up another: "Emilie, will you tell me a story, or shall I tell you one?"

This is Laurent the painter at his most vibrant; he is much more flamboyant than in the first *Bonhomme,* where only pinks colored the bold line drawings. Though still simple figures, Emilie and Bonhomme contrast with the elaborate, colorful world they encounter, dazzling in its shades of warm pinks, greens, blues, and purples against mostly white backgrounds. The fantasy is inventive, and some pictures are quite lovely: the pink house soaring above a green forest, Emilie dancing delicately on a roof while Bonhomme watches, and the Stone Horse disappearing over a pink mountain. Indeed, the book's most obvious appeal is its pictures, which bring Emilie and Bonhomme's stories to life.

The text, however, is much wordier and not as graceful as *Bonhomme*'s, and the rambly plot doesn't live up to its potential, relying more on visual episodes than on action or suspense. Bonhomme's wispy nature is nicely confirmed: he is a little coy, pettish, "loses his temper, . . . ties his spike into a knot," and again copes with sadness by going away. Yet he is still imaginative, whimsical, free-spirited, and tender. He and Emilie squabble but remain fast friends who understand and care about each other. But the refreshing uniqueness of this unusual character is lost, somehow, in all the rainbow-hued goings-on.

Though Laurent "didn't think of him as a child" (he translates "Bonhomme" as "good little man"), he is certainly worlds away from Babar. "Bonhomme has different possibilities," says the author. Indeed this blend of man and boy, realist and dreamer, is one of the artist's most complex—and probably most personal—characters, curiously believable because he is unclassifiable. He merged with the Wully-Wully in 1975, however, and was not heard from again.

Babar and the Wully-Wully

Wully-Wully, "an animal that is seldom seen," is like Bonhomme—gentle, shy, fun-loving, and free-spirited.[6] Instead of a single spike growing out of a bald head (or four antennae like the little blue dog of *Planet*), Wully-Wully has two leaf-ended sprigs, abundant hair, and a tail; his antagonists are enemy rhinos, not city officials, and he is the darling of all Célesteville, not just one little girl. But Wully is clearly a 1975 reincarnation of Laurent's favorite non-Babar protagonist, the first character linking his own stories to the Babars, and the stimulus for Flora to show her mettle in a well-plotted, exciting story.

The triplets just happen onto the "strange little animal" whom older residents welcome enthusiastically and seem to recognize. "'My goodness!' exclaims old General Cornelius, 'What an event! I haven't seen a Wully-Wully in almost ten years.'" (*Bonhomme* was published in 1965). At first, "Zephir the monkey acts reserved"; he has been, after all, the only nonelephant animal in the close family circle and is a practiced attention-getter himself.

But his pique is temporary, for Wully endears himself to the family with his fey behavior: he watches the children's electric train, fascinated "hour after hour"; he is uncatchable at hide-and-seek "because he makes no more noise than a feather"; he eats upside down, hanging by his tail from the chandelier; and the usually quiet creature amuses everyone when he "makes some loud squawks" on Arthur's saxophone.

But mean Rataxes, the old rhinoceros king, sees and wants Wully. "If I can snatch him away, he'll be mine!" Though Wully-Wully "lets out a piercing cry," he is powerless against the big rhino, who invades a pleasant picnic and carries him off in a sleek green car, "laughing loudly" and leaving the children "all in despair."

When Arthur and Zephir realize that Wully-Wully is "tied by a leash" and "looks very unhappy," they infiltrate the rhino city by posing as hat merchants. Arthur is recognized and imprisoned—but not clever Zephir; he twits and outwits the clumsy rhino guards and frees Arthur. Then, "quietly as a cat [he] creeps inside Rataxes' palace," right to the rhino's royal bedside, where he "takes the Wully-Wully in his arms and steals away as silently as he came in," fully redeeming his initial jealous impulses.

Everyone at home is overjoyed, especially Flora who has spent tearful days and sleepless nights worrying about her Wully-Wully. "Bravo, Arthur! Bravo, Zephir! . . . . You have outwitted Rataxes!" But not yet, for "suddenly—they hear a frightful rumbling like an earthquake!" In a powerful double spread of dust and movement, which Laurent says was motivated by the 1968

Sorbonne riots near his boulevard Saint-Germaine flat, the charging rhinos sweep vengefully through Célesteville, "carrying Wully-Wully away with them."

Public opinion is aroused. "The elephants are furious [and] want to fight." Babar, remembering another war with the rhinos, "does not want to go to war, but what can he do?" Tenderhearted Flora realizes that war might mean Wully-Wully "could be killed. And if he dies, there will be no more Wully-Wully." And so, armed with nothing but courage, and all alone, Babar's spunky little daughter confronts awesome Rataxes: "Why do you keep poor Wully-Wully in a cage? And why did you steal him? He is not yours." With her eloquent words about freedom Flora finally convinces the rhino king to let Wully-Wully "go where he wishes," and in so doing, saves not only Wully-Wully but "tame[s] the great, rough Rataxes" so completely that he lets Wully swing from his horn!

Illustrations are energetic and bright with interesting contrasts. Wully-Wully's welcoming day in Célesteville brings together all the main characters and settings for the only time in the Babar saga: Babar in green suit, bowtie, and crown; Céleste, the triplets, Arthur and Zephir, the Old Lady and Cornelius, Dr. Capoulosse, Poutifour the gardener, Olur the mechanic, Podular the sculptor; the Palais des Fêtes, gardens, desert hills, old thatched houses, and new ones with French-provincial roofs. Far from static, though, the scene moves from right to left, focusing on the fragile, inscrutable Wully-Wully perched on Babar's bulky knee. Later, the green and pleasant palace garden contrasts with Flora's tears, and Zephir's lightfooted antics are a foil for the rhino soldiers' bulky inertia. Energy virtually explodes from the red-and-black rhinoceros charge, buildings and uniforms reinforcing the rhinos' menacing indestructability. But reformed Rataxes is a study in pastel, lakeside calm after he capitulates to the adorable Wully-Wully.

Through interesting character contrasts, a de Brunhoff has again made important statements about war and peace, aggression and gentleness, weakness and power, freedom and responsibility. With fairytale clarity, Flora the small and weak is ultimately more powerful than Rataxes the big and strong. But her weapons are words not swords (or even tears); and, like an angel of happiness from *Babar the King,* she affirms that love and intelligence forge stronger bonds than anger and ignorance. Everyone is "bound to" Wully-Wully because "he is very gentle-looking and quite lovable," not just rare and exotic; he in turn is bound to the Célesteville and rhino friends who gave him independence—and with it responsibility and the obligation to visit those who love him.

Laurent has acknowledged that "there is something of myself in [Bonhomme] that is quiet and not overreacting to anything" and that Bonhomme "became Wully-Wully." By putting his own character into Babar's world, Laurent de Brunhoff has taken another step toward fully integrating his self with his legacy in a book that is Laurent-strong in every way.

Babar's Mystery

"Vacationing at the Grand Hotel" in Célesteville-on-the-Sea, the Babars are victims of mysterious thefts that lead them to Mont Saint Georges, which "at high tide . . . is surrounded by water—just like an island."[7] The mystery is ultimately solved at a lighthouse where the Old Lady is writing her memoirs to the sound of "nothing but the splash of waves and the cries of gulls." In a new (1978), bright "Big Babar," Laurent again, but more artistically than in *Babar's Castle* or *Babar Comes to America,* transforms real environments—the Riviera, Mont-Saint-Michel, lighthouses on Ile de Re and Montauk Point, Long Island, and his own phone number—into fictional images lively with color and real suspense.

Action begins in the first double spread with two figures, one in a checked cap, carrying a half-obscured piano from the Monaco-pink porch of the hotel. People "strolling on the promenade" are oblivious to the caper, but a crocodile in a green suit watches keenly from a window across the street. The plot thickens when Babar realizes that *their* "piano has been stolen! . . . Some furniture movers came to get it. . . . Nobody guessed that they were thieves!" The only clue is a glove that Flora finds on the sidewalk, but it is enough for detective manqué Arthur, a little bossy and self-important, to "start an investigation at once" and off they all go in search of a glove merchant whose shop is at the foot of Mont Saint Georges.

He can't help them, but while they are stopping "at an outdoor café to eat some delicious crêpes, a specialty of the region," Arthur spies what he considers an ominous-looking rhinoceros in a checked green suit and derby; "Do you think he might be one of the thieves?" But Babar and Céleste discount his suspicions, only to return to the parking lot and find that "someone has stolen [their] brand-new car." But who? A crocodile? a lion? surely not an elephant?

Having no luck at following a clue of their own, the triplets join the rest of the family at the Célesteville Seashore Grand Theater for the unveiling of a long-awaited statue of the elephant king. "Babar gives a sharp tug at the sheet, the cloth slides off. . . . NO STATUE! . . . Someone has stolen it!" The "crude dummy made from a barrel and some pieces of wood" is no substitute for the golden image of King Babar, and Arthur is galvanized once again into furious action as he follows "a red car speeding away" with "an enormous, peculiar-looking bundle" in the back seat.

He motorcycles to, of all places, the lighthouse where the Old Lady is working; nearby is a little shed from which Arthur hears laughter and music. "Sneak[ing] up quietly," he sees a piano, a red car, a golden statue, and four crocodiles, one in a checked cap and another in a green suit! When he pursues the group to a boat, they meet none other than the checked-suited rhino, a fence who gives them "half of the money" and a promise of "the rest when you deliver the loot at my place."

Finally Babar, who up to this time has been "in a state" or generally ineffectual, plans a thief-trapping strategy, that, with the Old Lady and Arthur's help, thwarts the quartet's nighttime crime and prompts crocodile tears. Even the rhino gang leader is nabbed in his getaway boat, to the delight of all who read the morning papers.

Beginning with a title page that shows everyone rushing somewhere, this story, one of Laurent's best plotted, moves with fast-paced action. The Old Lady's part is a little strained, as she seems only a device to introduce the lighthouse and her cat, an animal Laurent seldom draws.[8] And Babar is again disappointingly passive till the end, with the young people providing most of the verve. But unlike *Babar's Castle* and *Babar's Birthday Surprise*, readers know little more than the protagonists, and the suspense is engaging. Comfortable motifs like food at the Charcuterie d'Auvergne, courteous behavior ("we must not forget to take back some postcards for [the Old Lady]"), and rhino/crocodile villains give this vacation story a context of familiarity. Arthur is still a madcap motorcyclist but now wears a safety helmet.

Most pictures are filled with bright and sometimes clever detail: the lighthouse has a foreshadowing pulley system that is put to surprising uses; sea scenes are mouthwatering in clear blues, greens, and yellows; Mont Saint Georges is a stunning reprise of Mont-Saint-Michel, right down to tour buses and hillside shops; the nighttime landscape, with only a piercing lighthouse beacon to illuminate dark activities, is a well-balanced study in dramatic contrast; crooks are dressed in tasteless, gaudy clothes while, naturally, the Babars wear discreet resort whites.

Laurent's figures are solid, his black line heavier than usual; colors are flat but intense, giving the book a feeling of strong salt air rather than sweet lake breezes. Still a translation from his more spontaneous French, the text is awkward in spots and not as economical as it might be. And readers who continued to expect adherence to Jean's Babar tradition were generally unhappy. Nevertheless, Laurent's painting and storytelling are vigorous, and, if not profound in theme or character development, *Babar's Mystery* is suspenseful fun.

The One Pig with Horns

Ordinarily, it takes Laurent de Brunhoff a year or two from idea to book. *The One Pig with Horns* (1979), unique from the start, took 10.[9] When it finally appeared, interpretations were contradictory,[10] sensibilities were outraged, and sales were poor. In short, one of Laurent's favorite "very special" non-Babars, one he had supervised personally right down to the printing, was "not well received," probably because it in no way resembled the Babars.

Bursting out of the elephant utopia for what he says is the last time, Laurent has created a highly individual story about controlling destructive emotions and finding identity. With violent color and vehement line, he tells about a boastful but insecure pig who has "put horns on his forehead so as to be handsome as a bull." He has no sensitivity but plenty of touchiness and is envious of nearly everyone; "when you laugh at him he loses his temper," and then, literally, loses his head: "pig has exploded." Though he collects himself and tries other personalities—comedian, "lady pig," baby, flower—something always maddens him and "his head pops off again!" Finally his weary body rejects its hothead completely and becomes a grotesque with no identity at all. The head-with-the-horn cries "so hard and so long" from its disembodied perch in a tree that "the horns come unstuck," the head falls onto pig's shoulders, and "this time it will stay there for good." After wearing himself out with fury and fakery, pig accepts his own true hornless nature and transforms his anguish into art.

The power of this story about frustration depends, however, on much more than plot. Alternating between first-person assertions by pig and third-person narrative and commentary from a chorus of animal friends, the text is vibrant with expletives and conversational asides, forcing the reader to participate in its short-spurt energy. Pig is the essence of every role he tries: macho masculinity, always ready to shoot something; manic clownishness, providing his own laugh track; doting effeminacy, with wig, lipstick, and false eyelashes; bottle-sucking infancy, complete with babytalk. As a flower, he sprouts beautifully but when he "forgets just who he is," he's the epitome of furrowed-brow uncertainty. Pig works hard at self-denial!

Laurent shows these transformations with intense color and

line: pig literally winds up to explode, his pink head turning red like the sky and his eyes looking, appropriately, like mad bull's-eyes; at his most furious, he is a black-and-white shock of violent motion, head and body locked in a power struggle. But when he's playing calmer parts, pinks, aquas, blues, greens convey feeling, though neither color nor line is ever pastel or subdued.

Whether autoanalysis, as a friend of Laurent's humorously but perhaps tellingly suggested, or advice to youth, this last non-Babar is as far as possible from the elephant fantasy. "If you are driven by things and by events, like pig," says Laurent de Brunhoff, "that's bad." If you try to be what you are not, you'll explode—or implode; if, on the other hand, you find and accept yourself (as Laurent de Brunhoff the artist was beginning to do), with head and heart mutually in control, life can be rewarding and beautiful.

Babar's Little Library

Laurent underlines the world's beauty in *Babar's Little Library* (1980), a box of four exquisite, well-made, painter's books about the classical elements, published first by Diogenes.[11] Not stories, these are thoughtful, highly associative reflections on the nurturing sources of life—alternately humorous, cautionary, melancholy, practical, curious, wise, and reverential. Laurent considers it "one of my favorites, sort of a Zen meditation!" Yet its gentle ruminations are disarmingly childlike.

Familiar Babar characters and activities populate the tiny 2½-by-3½-inch, uncluttered pages where detail is not missed. Each delicate watercolor is balanced perfectly with words; the only improvement to the American edition would be a script, rather than print, text. Page design is pleasantly varied: sometimes a single-side picture is placed opposite words, sometimes there is a double spread; backgrounds are usually space-enhancing white, but occasionally blue. Some pictures are full of action; others are still. Often illustrations evoke other stories, especially those in the earlier, inferior boxed quartets of little books. But "About Air,"

"About Earth," "About Fire," and "About Water" are immeasura-
bly better because Laurent drew and wrote the books completely
himself.

"About Air" opens with a daydreaming elephant: "Lying on my
back I see a patch of blue sky and the clouds." It seems not to be
Babar, whose green suit and crowned head appear only on the
cover; in fact, the only visually individuated elephant in this meditation is Arthur. Instead, Everyman elephants muse on "Who
flies in the sky?" as they watch birds and butterflies, fly kites,
hold hats, and sweep wind-whirled leaves; one jousts at air-
driven windmills, another blows out candles, 'pfff!'"; still others
fill bubbles, balloons, trumpets, and bicycle tires with air. But
Arthur-Icarus finds that air won't hold elephants, except in a parachute, plane, or rocket. The most lyrical picture is the first of
elephant and clouds, with another "How lovely to fly above a sea
of clouds" nearly as good.

In "About Earth" Babar and Céleste contemplate along with
other elephants the potential of "wet," "heavy" earth for yielding
sculptures, vases, muddy footprints, and caves and for nurturing
seeds, trees, and indeed "everything, everywhere." Russets,
sands, and browns dominate—until the culminating double
spread where greens and pinks prove to be earthtones, too. The
potter at his wheel and Babar reading in the tree's "quiet shade"
are especially well designed.

In "About Fire," Babar strikes "a match. It bursts into flame"
and provides light and heat for candles, fireplace, campfire, cook-
ing, and manufacturing; it causes "commotion!" volcanoes, even a
dragon sting. But in a spectacular golden climax, fire is shown as
nurturer, too: "Please don't stand in my sunlight." Most pictures
are dramatic with reds and blacks, almost crackling; a lovely contrast are the pink-and-blue, bed-bound elephants holding their
golden flames as "the light of the candles dances on the walls."

"About Water" is, understandably, a book of blues and greens.
"There's really nothing better than fresh water" for drinking,
showering, bathing, splashing, fishing, diving, swimming, and
watering the garden; even rain is fine. Tears are salt water,
and so is the sea, not good for drinking or falling into unless one

is a whale. Coming from the elephant fountain of Castle Bonne-trompe, jetting water "sings its own song" and "still water is like a mirror." But, recalling Narcissus's fate, "don't lean over too far to look at yourself!" The energy in "when the sea is rough" is stunning for such a small picture; the diving sequence of "JUMP!", "Wheee!", and "SPLASH" is nicely tense; and the fishing double spread is a gem of gentle wit: "Fishermen *on* the water, fish *in* the water. One would dearly love to catch the other."

The little volumes celebrate nature with whimsical innocence, varying point of view as they go to include all readers. As fragile moments of concentrating, imagining, and feeling, they really defy explication. But like all good art, they rise above it as the whole transcends the parts.

Two Ghost Stories

The stimulus for *Babar and the Ghost* (1981), a little smaller than other mainstream Babars, was Laurent and Marie-Claude's fondness for gripping Gothic tales.[12] However, though there is plenty of action, there is little scary suspense. The old disarming immediacy and involvement is lost in a flat, past-tense translation by Random House editors. But most disappointing, after the stunning *Little Library,* is that Babar at his half-centennial is an unreflective, humorless, hyperrational shadow of his former self.

The family is on a hike to the Black Castle, but just as they get there, "a storm broke out. The sky grew dark and the wind began to howl." To avoid the rain, and against Cornelius's wishes, the family takes shelter in the castle that "looks haunted," only to find that it *is*—by "a white shape" that only the children can see. At first they catch just scary glimpses of the figure running down a vaulted hall and then emanating from a suit of armor. But when they finally meet the ghost, they find him friendly, urbane, and not a vampire, though he uses vintage Bela Lugosi dialogue: "Good evening. I am Baron Bardula." He regales them with castle lore, demonstrates the convenience of being ephemeral, and gets an invitation to "come with us to Célesteville."

He does. But in his quest for "good fun" he totally disrupts utopian life with spectral busyness, invisible to all adults as he pours lemonade, mows the lawn, harasses Cornelius, joins a family musicale, and foils the youngsters at hide-and-seek. Eventually the playful Baron goes too far even for Babar, who has insisted that "there is no such thing as a ghost." When a phantom blue car totally disrupts traffic—"The car had no driver!"—Babar pursues the speedster to the school playground and admonishes sternly, with some justification, "Ghost, if you are there, listen to me. . . . Go back to your castle." But only the children get a reply from the weary ghost. "I had a wonderful time, thanks to you, but . . . this lively life is tiring me out," whereupon "he faded into the night sky."

Illustrations in the first half do have a Gothic feeling: Black Castle, eerily empty against an ominous storm-sky, looks appropriately more like Castle Rackrent than Bonnetrompe. Bats, ravens, "mice and spiders" live amid cobwebbed, decaying grayblack architecture, which Laurent patterned after an eccentric English home he had read about; ghostly knights decorate the mantel; reds are dull, antique. Movement is minimal, the children rigid with fright in one picture. Only the doughy ghost seems mobile and unafraid in the darkness.

But in Célesteville, the atmosphere changes; pastoral scenes and colors dominate, and thanks to the antic phantom, so does action, climaxing in a daytime traffic jam that is a comic nightmare. The contrast of darkness and light is amusing as the nocturnal Baron tries life out of his element; like Bonhomme, he finds it ultimately wiser to go home where he can be himself.

The man so inventive with imaginary worlds is, commendably, celebrating children as special people, eagerly open to fantasy. But by having only the youngsters (and readers) see a ghost that adults are too opaque or rigid to believe in, Laurent removes suspense and demeans respected figures, forcing them out of character: sedate Cornelius, "the oldest and wisest of all the elephants" (King, 4, 5), is reduced to a querulous, timid grumbler "who hated mice and spiders." Babar has become a scoffer—

"Surely you don't believe in ghosts"—and a fool, imposing fatherly control only by denying the reality of the ghost. Even the Old Lady, who "cared so well for the wounded" (*Travels*, 47) after the bloody war with the rhinos, nearly faints at the ghost's tame tricks. The children behave uncharacteristically too, discourteous as "they whined, trying to sound like Cornelius" and laughed at the stupid adults.

Perhaps young readers enjoy seeing grown-ups powerless for a change. But irony does not fit into Babar's world where adults are models of benevolent authority for children who must learn the order of things. Apparently not intentionally, Laurent has made all the adults seem "a little bit silly." Worse yet, however, Babar the King has become just another fallible adult. Whatever the explanation, Laurent's usual humor has slipped into derision; the calm protagonist of *Babar's Little Library* has again become anxious.

Five years later, in 1986, an adaptation, *Babar and the Ghost: An Easy-to-Read Version*, was published for the very youngest readers "because Random House wanted a book for their collection Step into Reading rather fast." Laurent, whose life was in transition between France and America, had no time to finish a completely new story; however, because of language and layout constraints, he eventually recast the story extensively enough to make it seem almost new.

This version does a few things better. A peevish Cornelius and vaporish Old Lady are not part of the outing to Black Castle, though Babar and Céleste still insist that "there is no such thing as a ghost." Later on when the friendly phantom says, "But only you will see me. The grownups will not know I am around," and "[e]verybody laughed. What fun it was going to be!" it becomes clear that the fun will again be at adults' expense. But though the elephant king is still slow to understand that "something strange is going on," he does get the ghost's approval—"Your father is right. . . . It is time for me to go home," and Babar's sly smile on the last page hints that his mind is not so closed to fancy this time. The children are less disrespectful, more like their old food-

and fun-loving selves. And first glimpse of the ghost is delayed a bit, making for more suspense, at once frightening and reassuring for the children. "Please do not be scared. . . . I am a nice ghost."

But Laurent's ordinarily appealing light watercolor style is not vivid enough for a story inspired by Dracula. The Gothic atmosphere is gone, and Black Castle's only terrors are creaky floors and a skeleton staghead; the uniformly too-soft colors offer no visual shivers or witty contrasts. The action-packed traffic climax is reduced to everyday proportions and even the Baron's bounce seems deflated by the small pages. In a text done by editors, the past tense adds no vitality to short, controlled sentences and a vocabulary that is bland.

On its own, this easy reader may provide some do-it-yourself thrills for five-year-olds. But beside the original, which is itself not up to Babar par, it is undramatic, a decidedly earthbound ghost story.

Babar's Anniversary Album

Supervised and edited partially by Laurent, *Babar's Anniversary Album* (1981) is Random House's big (144 pages; 9-by-12-inch format) fiftieth birthday tribute to the beloved elephant.[13] Maurice Sendak's introduction is thoughtful and enlightening. Family photographs and glimpses of de Brunhoff art and creative process, all captioned informatively by Laurent, add a personal dimension hitherto unavailable in Babar criticism. The stories, Jean's first three and Laurent's best Célesteville stories with Random House, are well chosen. But in order to fit all this into a single volume, something had to be sacrificed. Unfortunately, it is the integrity of the stories themselves.

Hardest hit are Jean's 48-page "Big Babars." By cutting text and reducing or eliminating pictures, Random House editors have squeezed *The Story of Babar, The Travels of Babar,* and *Babar the King* into 23 pages each; *The Travels of Babar* is least damaged because Laurent eliminated the cannibal scene. But, even though the most famous double spreads are intact, the scope and scale of subtler pages, as well as their bits of visual humor, are lost. Tense is changed throughout to fit American storytelling conventions and so, "His name *was* Babar" (*Album,* 17), as if he were dead. Colors are brighter, harsher, especially in Jean's books, though story and picture in Laurent's *Babar's Birthday Surprise, Babar's Mystery* (why is it second?), and *Babar and the Wully-Wully* suffer in the same ways.

However commendable the original concept, this six-in-one album is not a fitting tribute to 50 years of de Brunhoff art. Beyond its helpful secondary information, the only advantage of this poorly reduced sampling of Babar is that it points readers to the original books.

A worthier part of the birthday celebration was the touring exhibit of 200 original de Brunhoff paintings, which, after its summer 1981 showing at Paris's Centre culturel de Marais, was acclaimed at nine American museums in 1983 and 1984 and yielded an informative catalog.[14]

The Concept Books

Laurent de Brunhoff had always defined himself as a painter, and in the early 1980s, he resumed personal painting after setting it aside to concentrate on a picture-book career. These three attractive volumes without stories gave his watercolor impulses free reign and saw King Babar resume his old role of benign inactivity.

Of course, Laurent's alphabet book is different from Jean's in style and substance. Random House decided not to publish *A.B.C. of Babar* in facsimile as they would Jean's other books, because of potential translation problems (though in 1936 they and Methuen had both successfully published an edition in English). Instead, they commissioned *Babar's A.B.C.* (1983), which gave Laurent "a rest—I did not have to invent a story"—and a palette nearly twice the size of Jean's.[15]

Rather than textless letter-vignettes with a glossary at the end, Laurent has chosen to combine visual and verbal examples for each letter. *A* is an "airport," complete with Flying Elephant Airlines; also, "Alexander aims his arrow at the apple"; and "Arthur plays an accordion." On the facing page, *B* shows Papa Babar with his three children; "the bear reads a book [titled *Babar*] in bed," and "the bird blows out the candles on the birthday cake" by fanning his wings.

The rest of the alphabet is represented by places, pastimes, and characters that evoke other de Brunhoff books: a circus ring, burning house, jungle, kitchen; ice skating, playing at the seashore, riding merry-go-rounds, driving cars, chasing butterflies; the extended family, rhinos, giraffes, kangaroos, lions, even a pig with no horns. But new personalities also liven the letters: a fox, koala, stork, opossum, reindeer, and rabbits. Unfortunately, there is no dog named Duck and children who know the dromedary camel conversation in *Babar's Fair*—"two humps of the camel . . . single hump of the dromedary" (19) may be confused when Laurent's "cat climbs onto the [one-humped] camel."

Like most alphabet picture books, this one confirms in a pleasant way what children already know about letter sounds. Some pictures have gentle humor: squirrels pelt a smelly skunk with acorns; orchestra members react with comic intensity to their musical task; a peacock is belle of the ball amid tuxedoed penguins; Arthur imitates a yawning yak. Other pictures are special for their art, particularly Laurent's adaptation of a unicorn tapestry, complete with orange and pomegranate trees on a field rouge. And *E* for elephant is an interesting variant of pages 4, 5, and 6 of *The Story of Babar*; the little elephants are rougher, though, and Mama carries birds on her back, not Bébé Babar.

The world Laurent draws is up to date, with zippered sleeping bags, X rays, lift-top vans, television sets, and helicopters; the style he uses is crisp and modern. Some readers might wish for less clutter or more unity and emotional depth to each picture. Luckily, the two *A.B.C.* books do not cancel one another; if Laurent's is not as imaginatively stimulating as Jean's, it is nevertheless visually engaging.

To achieve even better the light, airy effect he wanted for his fantasy worlds, Laurent changed the reproduction method in his next book, beginning now with transparent watercolor over a

spontaneous pencil sketch, and adding the traditional black out-
line later on with an acetate overlay. Fittingly, he launched the
experiment in *Babar's Book of Color* (1984), a rainbow tour de
force that dazzles the eye.

"One morning when Babar is painting in his studio, surrounded
with tubes of oil color and waiting canvasses," the children ask,
"Please, Papa, may we have some of your paints?" Babar gives
them "a bucket of red, yellow, and blue, and a little bit of black
and a little bit of white," and from these basics they create brilliant double-spread fantasies, at the same time showing child
readers how to mix colors.

Flora, no longer dressed in pink, paints a large lobster in her
favorite color, bold red; Pom imagines a blue whale and "paints a
pale blue sky" while adventurous Alexander chooses yellow for
his swarm of single-minded bees. The secondary colors define a
great green crocodile flanked by frogs, nine fat orange pumpkins,
and Queen Celeste driving a car of various hues of purple. Pom's
black crows seem to have enough power to handle a predatory cat,
but the white polar bears are too benign to scare anyone, especially with Babar the snowman eyeing them. More color mixes
show a herd of undressed, and therefore not from Célesteville,
gray elephants, some gangly pink flamingos, a brown teddy-look-
ing bear, and a tan camel that still has only one hump. At the end
Babar tests the children to see if they can name the colors they
have made, a disappointingly limp wrap-up of the foregoing free-
spirited pages.

Unencumbered with story, Laurent revels in large, clean
shapes and colors set against uncluttered white backgrounds. But
for all their simplicity, the pictures have wit: Babar portraits Céleste as Renaissance royalty; the lobster looks lively, but young
gourmet Alexander reminds everyone that "lobsters are always
red—after they are cooked!"; the scuba-diving elephant's flip-
pered "feet" and swimming "hands" and trunk replicate in mini-
ature the movements of the great whale; a royal mechanic
lounges while he sybaritically nibbles grapes; one polar bear skis
stylishly, without poles, but the mislabeled camel looks too sleepy
to go anywhere.

In all the paintings there is a pleasant feeling of immediacy, with the short text once more in present tense and the children just finishing each picture. *Babar's Book of Color* does not advance the Babar saga but it does foreshadow Laurent's style and content for the decade's balance, as Babar commands, if not center stage, at least a dignified cameo role.

Thanks to the new reproduction technique and Laurent's transparent pastel watercolors, *Babar's Counting Book* (1986) maintains the airy lightness of its opening page. As in *Babar's Book of Color*, the triplets are at home in Babar's studio; this time Céleste is in person, comfortable in a cane chair, while Zephir peeks in from the pink-floored palace porch just outside. A blue-green European shutter is flapping; a bird flies over pink hills into blue sky. The children want Babar to "come outside" to see them count, but the reader is already there, feeling the summer warmth that the pictures capture so well.

From one to ten, the children show that they are indeed good counters: one familiar red-billed marabou; two bright balloons big enough for Pom, Flora, and Zephir to travel in; three fast red cars, racing "Whoosh! Whoosh! Whoosh!"; four round purple hippos contrasting nicely with four spiky palm trees; five gentlemen alligators interestingly on the run; six ostriches running from them; seven elephants saved from the rain by red, white, and blue umbrellas; eight noisy blue parrots; nine tan camels (really dromedaries), eight benign and one feisty; and ten flying storks following a talkative leader's directions. Right along, Zephir pops up in unexpected places to keep the count.

"Babar is very proud of his children," and so is the young reader when he can count each group in a busy double-spread panorama of Lake Célesteville: How many alligators are there? How many balloons? How many snails creeping by? Children then learn to count from 10 to 20 by addition in a picture that could have been monotonous but isn't because each animal is individuated. Finally, successful achievement is rewarded by a royal certificate, the first document with Babar's official seal since the triplets' birth, proclaiming "that you have learned to count to 20." As reinforcement, even the endpaper elephants are numbered. With no story demands, Laurent the nature painter and gentle wit is enjoying himself thoroughly. A new serenity of color, subject, and line marks this book, conceived in France but completed in Middletown, Connecticut.

Laurent's change of personal milieu when he was 60 affected the substance as well as the style of his art. Babar, who was an anxious, aging antagonist in the last mainstream story (*Ghost* 1), became a more benign but minor figure in the concept books. However, after his private renaissance, Laurent was emboldened to cast the elephant king once again in an important, if not primary, role—and to revitalize Babar tradition with fresh spirit.

Babar's Little Girl

"The little girl which I created [in America], Isabelle, is the final touch of an evolution." For Laurent "a new life was coming. The same could happen with Babar. Babar could have a new life too!" In *Babar's Little Girl* (1987), eagerly anticipated, well-publicized, and enthusiastically received, Laurent fully captures the "rebirth" spirit and reaches the height of his individuality.[16] His watercolor landscapes are even more luminous; he brings another old non-Babar character comfortably into the elephant world. And, happily contradicting himself—"I never want to add permanent characters to the Babar family" (*Album*, 14)—he invigorates the royal household with a lively new child named, not after the monkey princess he didn't like (*Zephir*), but for his own intrepid niece, Isabelle, whom he admired very much.

Action begins with the title page, as the whole extended family focuses on Céleste, "who was going to have another baby!" Her pregnancy is clearly shown and described: "Celeste was heavy and round. She got tired easily." There is no mincing of words about the delivery, either: "All of a sudden she called out to Babar, 'Quick! Get Doctor Capoulosse. . . . The baby is about to arrive!' But before the doctor could get there, the baby was born," under a tree. To Babar's delight, "It was a girl."

Comparison with *Babar and His Children* is inevitable, and

Laurent relies on readers' memories of Jean's story to individuate the decidedly modern Isabelle. She is indeed an "amazing baby," exceptional in every way: she does not choke on her rattle like Flora; she is not as greedy as Pom, though "her appetite was astonishing." Yet she is as physically rambunctious as Alexander. In fact, everyone is so "enchanted" and "proud of her" that she commands the head of the table at a low-cholesterol family breakfast and at her own spectacular birthday party when she gets bigger (which she does quickly because Laurent did not want "to do *Babar and His Children* again").

But Isabelle is reflective and kind, too; she observes a grasshopper quietly, and politely rescues a turtle and then a cat. She loves music in live performance and on earphones; and the limber little elephant is a skillful roller skater. Like all children, she suffers an occasional, deserved scolding and sometimes loses herself in play and imagination.

On one such occasion while walking with the family, she completely forgets the time: "She wandered farther and farther until she reached the Blue Valley," a paradise of green-blue mountain peaks, soft trees, sandy beaches—and the home of two "friends of the family," the cultivated "gentlemen" Boover and Picardee. To Isabelle's conversational overture, "I am looking for someone to play with," the pair replies, "You've come to the right place." And so it is: the three snack on juice and cookies, play a challenging game of hide-and-seek, and improvise jazz. The hosts teach Isabelle how to do yoga (which Laurent has practiced since 1974), play poker, and tap dance. And through it all, the ageless pair has as much fun as she.

But when they watch evening television, "there was Babar on the screen!" informing viewers that "our little girl has disappeared. . . . Isabelle, if you are listening, please come home right away." As tender as she is lively, the little elephant regrets worrying her family—"I did just what Papa told me not to do"—and with Boover and Picardee's help, literally flies home to her faintly envious siblings and her "grateful," loving parents.

Laurent made Isabelle a girl of the 1980s—slimmer than her rotund siblings ("to make her different," says Laurent), self-con-

Isabelle was overjoyed with her birthday presents—a pair of roller skates and a cassette player with earphones. While out for a spin on her new skates, she noticed a cat up in a tree. She thought it was lost.

"Kitty, come down," she called. "I will help you."

But the cat stayed right where it was. Isabelle waited and waited until the cat made up its mind to come down.

Isabelle tries out her birthday presents. From *Babar's Little Girl* by Laurent de Brunhoff. Copyright © 1987 by Laurent de Brunhoff. Reprinted by permission of Random House, Inc.

fident, fearless—in fact, almost too venturesome for even a fantasy five-year-old. Yet child she is, adored and pampered by her family but needing guidance and warm, end-of-day security in spite of her independence. Babar regains his strong, sweet nature and, like a good father, shies neither from disciplining nor loving little Isabelle, about whom he is clearly dotty. In the background, as he is in most of Laurent's stories, he is nevertheless once again the substantial parent who feelingly echoes sentiments spoken 50 years earlier, "Truly it is not easy to bring up a family. . . . But how nice the babies are!" (*Children*, 40).

Boover and Picardee are urbane bons vivants who share a lovely white Victorian house that is a cross between Chessy and the president's home at Wesleyan University, down the street from Laurent in Middletown. Boover is plump and resembles a nattily dressed dog, clever but not as physically adept as bow-tied Picardee who looks like a gangly, two-legged camel and first appeared as Laurent's persona in *A tue-tête* 30 years earlier. They enjoy hide-and-seek with Isabelle as much as sophisticated pastimes; in fact, their life is too full to accommodate short-notice meetings with the king and queen, making Isabelle's adventures with the young-hearted bachelors entirely her own.

Like *Babar's Counting Book,* the pictures reflect Laurent's new working method and his return to personal watercolor painting, an artistic outlet clearly important to him but neglected for many years. Sturdy elephants are drawn with a delicate line that is airy against pastel backgrounds. Detail is minimal, which may disappoint veteran Babar lookers, but in lyrically uncluttered pictures like the double spread of Blue Valley and the aerial view of Célesteville, now an even bigger city, small visual distractions are not missed. Blue Valley is, in fact, the dream impetus for the story, for Laurent had always wanted to paint the strange pyramid mountains of Chuanyen, China, that he knew only from a postcard. His new Eden, within walking distance of Célesteville, has whimsically incompatible trees, a New England house improbably overlooking a river populated by hippotami, and an aged elephant ferryman who, Charon-like, rows Isabelle across the river to new adventures. As always, though, Laurent blends fantasy and realism when, earlier, Céleste removes her crown for Isabelle's delivery.

The text, even in past tense, is melodious. Though entirely fluent in English, Laurent still writes most spontaneously in French, which in this case, Phyllis Rose (herself a writer and Laurent's second wife) translated and, along with Random House editor Jane O'Connor, helped polish. The plot is logical and exciting, beginning and ending with warm home scenes. Isabelle is a delightful combination of modern and traditional female and self-sufficient and dependent child. Babar is an up-to-date father, overtly affectionate and no longer bound by the conventional limits of male parenting that influenced Jean's portrait of the new father Babar in *Babar and His Children*. But the importance of fun and freedom bolstered by family discipline and love is an old de Brunhoff theme that Laurent sounds at the peak of his creativity when he is "perfectly free to do what I [want]"—and does.

More Isabelle Stories

Predictably, just as youthful Laurent made "brother" Arthur his chief protagonist, mature Laurent now focuses fondly on "granddaughter" Isabelle in simple, youthfully spirited stories for young readers.[17]

Fifty-one years after Jean's *Daily Sketch* serial, "Babar and Father Christmas," Laurent offers a Christmas narrative that features the newest Babar offspring. Readers may regret, however, that "Christmas with Babar and Baby Isabelle" (1987) was published in a (also Hachette-owned) magazine rather than as a book. Unfortunately, it too is in the past tense.

Conflict is foreshadowed from the beginning: Isabelle wants to help Babar cut a Christmas tree in the forest, but though she bravely plods on, her "skis are too small" and "her feet hurt" (61). Readers who know how necessary skis are to the Babars in winter read on to discover how Isabelle gets a pair that fits. The suspense is nicely sustained as the family first trims the tree with bright, homemade decorations. That done, Babar sends the children to bed to wait for Santa Claus, "but Isabelle [can't] sleep" (63) and instead creeps down the stairs to look at the tree once more before morning.

In her excitement, though, she sees something that frightens her, falls—"Down [comes] Isabelle, down [comes] the ladder, down [comes] the Christmas tree!" (63)—and wakens her parents. "I saw a monster with horns and big teeth" (64), she tells Babar. And she is worried that Santa will "take back her presents because she [has] knocked down the tree" (64). But Babar, ever reassuring, tells her that there is no monster—only shawl-draped "new, *bigger* skis for Isabelle!" (64). In a faintly (but unintentionally) Christian-sounding finale, little readers are reassured that Santa bears no grudges: "He will forgive you, as I do, because trees are not the most important part of Christmas. Love is" (64).

Illustrations are in luminous watercolor, as bright as the season. Isabelle carries herself with perky assurance until, childlike, she needs her mother's comfort, though in the picture, Céleste's cradling looks anything but comfortable. A faceless, monster *shadow* would perhaps have made for better visual suspense, and, of course, book format would have given more leisure to the design; as it is, pictures and text are too crowded.

Still, this is another sprightly glimpse at how Isabelle is becoming the focal point of Babar's life, bringing out further the fatherly tenderness that had been effectively dormant since *Babar and His Children* and expanding the saga for a younger audience.

Babar's Little Circus Star (1988) is the second "Step into Reading" Babar, "with . . . very large type and extremely simple vocabulary, . . . created for the very youngest," even more basic than *Ghost* 2. Verbal information is minimal in this story of fewer than 300 words, with sentences rarely more than 10.

Because she is excluded from her siblings' activities, Isabelle, "the baby of the family" (5), is tired of "being so little" (*Star,* 6). Not until she has shown her mettle—and worn herself out—as a circus clown and daredevil is she ready to accept that "sometimes it is nice to be little!" (32). The text, written mostly by Random House editor Jane O'Connor (who had also worked on *Babar's Little Girl*), is musically cadenced with balanced words and phrases, not an easy task at such a basic reading level; as a narrative, the story has well-shaped dramatic action and a pleasing conclusion.

Laurent's airy watercolors confirm but also elaborate on the plot, especially in the circus settings and moments of action: his elephant clowns are bright and goofily dressed; Isabelle is a dazzling headliner in starry tights and egret-feather crown and executes flips gracefully. The double-spread circus-ring scene, with background spectators watching the central arc of action, invites comparison with the more complex one in Jean's *The Travels of Babar* and epitomizes the difference between de Brunhoff the father of 1932 and de Brunhoff the son of 1988: Jean's circus is detailed, witty, but dramatically serious; Laurent's is less minutely concentrated and lighter-hearted.

This third story exploring Little Isabelle's well-bred but independent nature has enough feminism and fantasy to satisfy the empathetic daydreams of even today's preschoolers. But though she is a very modern little girl, Isabelle comes happily back to the nurturing family environment where "everybody loves her—Babar most of all" (*Star*, 5). In its simple way, *Babar's Little Circus Star* is successfully contemporary and yet satisfyingly traditional.

With *Babar's Busy Year*, published in 1989, 16 years after *Meet Babar and His Family*, Laurent has produced another young readers' book of seasons; this one is a little larger, hardbound and has cardboard pages, but like the first, it is filled with sensory pleasures and family warmth that is "just right for 2's and 3's."

Rather than with a spring orchard this book begins, surprisingly, and not to be understood until the end, with Isabelle's announcement to Babar and Céleste that "the leaves have turned red and yellow. And they are starting to fall." She joins her siblings and cousin Arthur in a variety of autumn pleasures: hopscotch, soccer, harvest, and Halloween. When winter comes, Cornelius and the Old Lady prefer knitting and reading in front of the fire, but the family "goes to the mountains. They enjoy skiing and sledding." Still, Flora joyously greets spring's cherry blossoms; Arthur, Zephir, and Isabelle love its daffodils, tulips, and baby birds; Babar plants his beloved garden and welcomes the rain. Summer brings "picnics by the lake," bug hunts, and such perfect, cooling swims that Arthur wants it to "last forever." But not Isabelle. "I want fall to come again. I get to go to school. And I can't wait!" The book ends with Isabelle and Babar setting off the first day of school—with umbrellas and anticipation.

Like Laurent's other books for very young listeners or readers, this text is a collaboration between the artist and his editor, simple, but considering the short sentences, not monotonous. Word choices are vivid enough for toddler imaginations—"cool and tingly," "sunny and warm"—and short interjections draw readers in—"What a spooky face!" "Look at all that snow!" As is common in Laurent's stories, the title is slightly misleading; Babar is hardly the major protagonist—perhaps *The Babars' Busy Year* would have been more accurate. As always, picture messages subtly extend plot and character development: apparently, Isabelle is too little for skiing and swimming because her distinctive figure does not join Arthur's and the triplets', but she leads the way on other outings and knows how to entertain herself.

Very much a product of Laurent's lighter style and reproduction technique, the painting is breezy, with mellower colors and more white space than *Meet Babar and His Family*. It reveals a calmer, more reflective de Brunhoff, and a softer world with fewer details and activities. Most of the time, the sweet leisure of *Babar's Busy Year* compares favorably, picture by picture, with the earlier almanac. But occasionally one cannot smell the air quite so well: the 1989 cherry trees "burst into bloom" but the 1973 orchard shows it more dazzlingly; the rusty fall forest that opens the new story misses the brilliant intensity, the chill bite of fall that epitomizes autumn in the older one. Still, this is a quietly satisfying trip with familiar friends through another idyllic year.

At one time, Laurent had in mind to create a strong female villain, a sort of rhinoceros Lady MacBeth. However, "I don't know how to be mean," he has commented, and instead he made *Isabelle's New Friend* (1990), in which Mrs. Rataxes is a narrow-minded, overprotective mother whose son, nevertheless, becomes Isabelle's best and lasting friend.

The setting is Rhino City, not seen since *Babar and the Wully-*

Wully and depicted as still a little racist: "An elephant in Rhino City? How *very* strange!" (8). The cast is complete with old favorites like Babar and Céleste, Cornelius, King Rataxes, and a new helpful hippo, Murphy Heavybottom. In a nicely paced plot, the youngsters have "lots of fun together" (7), sharing childish adventure and then danger. But the too-conservative adults are tentative about the unorthodox relationship, and parental hysteria nearly takes over when the children are lost. All ends well, however, and wise Babar acknowledges that Vic Rataxes really "is a nice little boy" (31).

In attractive, interesting scenes, Laurent is gently urging tolerance and championing the innocent wisdom of children. Very different from his opaque adult self in *Babar and the Ghost*, Babar is a happier, more flexible parent who understands and cares about but does not coddle his favorite child. Even-tempered Céleste is patient with old Cornelius's initial reaction to little Vic: "Long ago there was a war with a rhinos. . . . Cornelius thinks all rhinos are bad—big or small." The Heavybottoms are kind, if unimaginatively named, friends. But Lady Rataxes, angry to the end, exudes potential villainy in her red and black outfit and (probably) fake eyelashes.

Generally, though, the tones are soft and their watercolor origin is obvious. Sometimes the smaller pages seem a little busy with events. But the occasional double spreads—the title page, the parents' confrontation, and, most spectacular, the storm scene that is so reminiscent of *Babar's Picnic*—mitigate the clutter. Isabelle is as appealing as ever, following in her sister Flora's rhino-tolerant footsteps, crying not for timidity but for joy as she greets Vic, "My friend!"

The Babar Calendars

Some of Laurent's most personally satisfying and artistically representative original work in recent years has been the calendars he compiled in the late 1980s. Shown in a 1989–90 exhibition at the Mary Ryan Gallery in New York (the last stop in the 1983–84

American tour), the 1989 and 1990 calendar paintings are an essential part of his creative output. Like Jean's *A.B.C. of Babar,* the calendar pictures are wordless vignettes that feature Babar in various activities and wittily expand his world and personality. The first calendar, *Babar's Adventures, 1988 Calendar,* is almost exclusively favorite double spreads from both de Brunhoff's works, brightly reproduced in 16-by-11½-inch, larger-than-original glory. The only new work by Laurent is a cover and centerfold, though the rest of the pictures are among the best of earlier de Brunhoff originals.

But for *Babar's Adventures, 1989 Calendar,* Laurent created all-new pictures that feature Babar at appropriate seasonal sports. The watercolor is light and transparent, particularly lovely in the huge balloon centerfold, the canoe-in-the rapids cover, and the watery scuba scene. Other pictures are full of charm and wit: Babar has thumbs in his ski mittens, plays basketball with the grace of a dancer, roller skates and windsurfs like a professional. He even tries polo, to the slight discomfort of the horse who probably weighs less than he. Though he doesn't always wear his crown, the unmistakable badge of office is somewhere on his person at every event. A few small, unidentified pictures, some from even Jean's stories, sprinkle the monthly pages and each sporting event is captioned to relate to and extend life in Célesteville.

In even farther fetched illustrations, in 1990 Laurent imagines *Babar in Hollywood,* starring the elephant king in some of the great films, past and present. There are classics like "Farewell to Babar" (*A Farewell to Arms*), "Captain Babar" (*Captain Blood*), "Ben Babar" (*Ben Hur*), and more modern hits like "Top Ton" (*Top Gun*), "Road Warrior Babar," and "Wolfgang Amadeus Babar." The stirring centerfold has "Beau Babar" (*Beau Geste*) in French Legionnaire uniform, trumpeting a rhino charge while Arthur, the script boy, and Zephir, the wind man, watch with the rest of the crew. "Minnesota Babar" (*The Hustler*) is properly Gleasonesque in windowpane suit and red bowtie but skillful with his royal cue. "Babar in Space" is so scary that the triplets lose their popcorn and Cornelius his glasses. Bikinied "Beach Blanket" Céleste is a sight to behold and the Fred and Ginger royals on the cover could make a living at ballroom dancing.

Like a good revisionist, in 1991 Laurent rewrites the story of America in *Babar in History.* Heretofore unrecorded, Babar arrives (with Rataxes) at Ellis Island, pans for gold in the California Gold Rush, helps build the Brooklyn Bridge, stars at Woodstock, and runs for president. He is on hand as the first elephant to sign the Declaration of Independence, discover electricity, fly the Wright Brothers' plane, co-invent the telephone with Alexander Graham Bell, and cross the Delaware. Céleste celebrates the Nineteenth Amendment with other suffragettes; Cornelius and Rataxes, friends once, toast the connection of the East-West railway. In a picture reminiscent of but not humorous like the American Gothic Babar poster that Laurent did for the Cedar Rapids Museum opening of the 1983–84 traveling exhibit, the Dust Bowl Babars sadly bid farewell to their farm. And Babar takes "one small step for an elephant, a giant step for elephantkind" (July) as he plants his species print on the moon; here readers cannot but remember *Babar's Moon Trip* and delight in Laurent's *original* painting of the event. This almanac is a lighthearted rampage through history by a Frenchman who loves to chuckle at his adopted land as much as he did in *Babar Comes to America*—but knows it better.

Although not narratives, these calendars contribute to the Babar saga in much the same way as Laurent's "concept" books—by showcasing characters in amusing, imaginative, original ways. Of course Babar's public always hopes for a new big book, and Laurent hints that one is in progress.

Whatever the final form of the next de Brunhoff Babar, the elephant king will be benignly back in control, if not constantly in evidence, in a utopia that is modern but still traditional and "filled with love and understanding." After 45 years, Laurent de Brunhoff has achieved his own kind of artistic identity and serenity, where "everyone [particularly the artist] is happy" once more.

Conclusion

There are readers today, not only children, who are unaware that the Babar stories are the work of two men. But though father and son share name and background, their art and storytelling are quite different. Clearly Laurent is not Jean. And yet after 60 years Babar is still Babar, thanks to the strength of one man's creation and the commitment of the other to keeping it alive.

Jean de Brunhoff is considered by some to be the father of modern picture books; thus, his influence on fellow visual artists other than his son is inescapable, going far beyond the specific cases already cited. Both de Brunhoff text and illustration has provided a benchmark of excellence for story makers like Maurice Sendak, who readily acknowledges his debt (*Album*, 11–14). The message of optimistic perseverance that Jean de Brunhoff articulated is echoed in many children's books, even subtle, recent paeans to hopeful determination like Arthur Yorinks' *Hey Al*. Though no other animal saga is so long-lived, the Babars have provided a pattern for anthropomorphized creatures like Russell Hoban's Frances, the little badger; James Marshall's George and Martha, the huge hippos; Else Minarik's Little Bear; Arnold Lobel's Frog and Toad; and a host of other family-centered picture book series that gently and amusingly socialize children into worthwhile values and behavior.[1] As a truly international character, Babar continues to be a unique ambassador of world peace, gentility, and benevolence, kept vital in translations of Jean's classic message-minded stories and Laurent's contemporary flights of fancy.

Jean's seminal, child-directed stories are indeed modern fables, richer in character and setting than traditional animal stories but as strong in theme. Rather than merely commenting on human behavior, Jean shows how grown-up life can and ought to be.

151

Never moralistic, he is nonetheless serious about creating a model world in which happy endings come not from magic intervention but from behavior based on logic and love. That his "grown-ups" are elephants who have animal as well as human traits only adds to his solid purpose and delightfully incongruous humor—and to readers' willing suspension of disbelief.

Like his countrymen La Fontaine and Perrault, Jean de Brunhoff is a storyteller urbane enough to fascinate and teach adults, despite the judgment of the first American to review the stories.[2] But his utopia is made first for children, filled as it is with adventures and details, characters and ideas that invariably engage but never condescend to them: births, ceremonies, cars, costumes, food, play, travel; accidents, mischief, sorrow, danger, even death; model adults, loving discipline, close family, stable home. His humor is accessible, and even though children may not recognize that an elephant statue in *Babar the King* is based on *Diana* by Desjardins in the Allée of the Three Fountains at Versailles, they can enjoy its bulky dignity.

If Jean's first story was for his own sons, the rest were for all children; he was a universal father, unabashedly sharing his personal hopes, strategems for living, and pleasures. The elephant world is crowded with what C. S. Lewis would call "the habitual furniture" of Jean de Brunhoff's mind and the "spiritual roots"[3] he struck during his life. The Babars are lasting and powerful because they are his storied ideals.

But Babar was Jean's persona, not Laurent's. As a very young man, he chose to perpetuate a creation that was beloved by him but was not his. The challenge, he would realize, was to find his own voice and authenticate the legacy for himself. Jean had fully formed Babar; had clearly articulated the philosophical, social, and political systems of his utopia; had illustrated a physical environment that apparently wanted for nothing. Where could Laurent go?

"Father-faithfulness" was not an ongoing option, for Laurent was soon too old to be just son—and too different. From the start, his pictures had a less child-centered point of view and detail; his brush stroke was more kinetic and thus harder to reproduce well than Jean's. His stories often lacked drama and rambled episod-ically; his main characters, being children, were action-oriented and had limited chance to show the reflective depth of Jean's thoughtful protagonist. He had fairly classic French bourgeois ideas about behavior but didn't use them as story themes; be-sides, Jean had said most of the important things, and Laurent was more than a mimic.

He was, in fact, a painter and a dreamer; from that talent and nature came *his* Babar strength and originality: he drew places and imagined environments that far exceeded his father's domes-tic imaginings—a bigger Célesteville, the world beyond, outer space, and eventually lands of pure fancy. When he couldn't de-velop main characters any further, he altered their roles, modi-fied their importance, and focused on the children's growth. He created unusual individuals of his own, too, and after 40 years, fit one nicely into the nuclear Babar family. Consistent with his emphasis on young protagonists, he shaped the stories for readers of even two and three, broadening the audience (if limiting the substance) of the books. In short, Laurent has accepted the obli-gation to vitalize Babar in his own best way; free from merely replicating Jean's utopia, he now sounds new themes in his own, more sophisticated style, from "spiritual roots" that encompass more than the first 12 idyllic years of his life.

"Something that comes out of my stories is some kind of love and understanding of the other. That is essential to me. Every-body trusts anybody. Maybe it's foolish; maybe it's not the real world, especially today when there is so much tension and fear. I don't want anything of that kind to appear in my books. Maybe it's utopia. But it's the kind of dream kids need. I want kids to dream and to travel in their imagination." As Arthur Applebee carefully demonstrates,[4] children's expectations from and ideas about life are patterned early, and though Laurent often denies having a message in his stories, he is clearly showing young read-ers how to dream—which is exactly what his father advised nearly 60 years ago in *Babar the King*.

Jean created one kind of dream, Laurent another. While serv-ing his own art and nature, the son built on images and meanings in the father's stories. But to insist on a "father standard" is futile and foolish, for the men and their times are different. As John Newbery, the first publisher of children's literature knew in the eighteenth century—and as generations of de Brunhoffs know in the twentieth—publishing is a business as well as an art. Babar has endured for 60 years because he is personable *and* profitable. Jean's most important books were launched by his own family, publishers traditionally as sensitive to artistic priorities as to business interests. Laurent, however, had to adapt his creativity to a publishing milieu that, perhaps for defensible fiscal reasons, sometimes seemed more commercial than aesthetic.

Without Jean de Brunhoff's creative intelligence, of course, there would be no dignified, sensible, benevolent Babar. But though Laurent has inevitably modernized, extended, and sometimes even disrupted the idyll, he has ultimately honored his legacy. In de Brunhoff Babars, the elephant utopia is intact. Babar the King—and all he stands for—reigns secure. Long live happiness!

Babar forever! From *The Story of Babar, the Little Elephant* by Jean de Brunhoff. Copyright 1937 by Random House, Inc. Reprinted by permission of Random House, Inc.

Notes and References

Preface

1. See Perry Nodelman, *Words about Pictures* (Athens, Ga.: University of Georgia Press, 1988), for the most comprehensive study to date on the way pictures make meaning.

2. Nicholas Fox Weber, *The Art of Babar* (New York: Abrams, 1989); hereafter cited in text. Discrepancies between original and reproduced art are revealed throughout Weber's book but explained on p. 185.

3. Charles I. Mundale, "Of Matthew Mallard, King Babar, and the Politics of Architecture," *Twin Cities Magazine,* December 1983, 85.

4. Accenting in Random House Babars is confusingly inconsistent: Céleste is accented in *The Story of Babar, The Travels of Babar,* and *A.B.C. of Babar* but not in the rest of Jean's or any of Laurent's books, although "Célesteville" appears in a picture in *Babar's Fair.* Zéphir is accented in *A.B.C.* and *Babar and Father Christmas* but, curiously, not in *Zephir's Holiday* or any of Jean's or Laurent's other books. "Cornélius" appears in *A.B.C.* but nowhere else. It is "Eléanore" in *Holidays* but "Eleanor" in *Babar's Cousin: That Rascal Arthur.* As noted, I keep the French spelling of Céleste and Célesteville but do not accent Zephir or Cornelius. To make matters even more confusing, the English editions from Methuen have no accents at all!

Chapter One

1. My correspondence with Laurent de Brunhoff goes back to fall 1987 (prior to that time, questions were addressed to him through Ole Risom at Random House). I had the additional advantage of many phone conversations from July 1989 to April 1991 and an interview with M. de Brunhoff in Middletown, Connecticut, on 7 and 8 October 1989.

2. See Edwin McDowell, "Babar at 50," *New York Times,* 20 November 1981.

3. For Jean's elephant designs see Weber, 1–9; for specifics on *Normandie,* see John Maxtone-Graham, *The Only Way to Cross* (New York: MacMillan, 1972).

4. In 1969 the French Télé-Hachette made a television series about Babar, using live actors in costume, a cumbersome medium for bulky Babar. A literary spin-off over which Laurent had only minimal control was *Le Journal de Babar* published in France in the early 1970s; Laurent designed one or two short stories for what was otherwise a reading-activity book done by others. For Laurent's earliest U.S. product endorsements, see "Babar: The de Brunhoff Books for Children," *Publishers Weekly*, 20 November 1961, 17–20.

5. *Babar: The Movie* (1989), Nelvana Entertainment, Toronto; merchandising rights by Clifford Ross Co., Los Angeles. Reactions to the film are mixed, but animated elephant comedies all evoke Disney. During the promotion of the film, Laurent commented, "I have not the final word but I know what they are doing. I do make comments . . . [but] I didn't create anything." Fond of animation and movement, as his work shows, he thinks "it's very well done" for a medium so differently paced from the picture book and helped promote the film. In the late 1980's, however, Ross sued Nelvana for contract violations ("milking the elephant" and "failing to consult"). Laurent keeps above the legal fray as Nelvana-Ross "spin offs" continue to proliferate. See David Margolick, "Lawyer in Celesteville? Babar Is in Court," New York *Times*, 30 September, 1990, 1.

6. For an apt sociological study of *le foyer* and French milieu, see Rhoda Metraux and Margaret Mead, *Themes in French Culture: A Preface to the Study of the French Community*, Hoover Institute Studies, Series D (Los Angeles: Stanford University Press, 1954). For a bourgeois French-American's candid view of his own people, see Sanche de Gramont, *The French: A Portrait of a People* (New York: G. P. Putnam's Sons, 1969). For an exhaustive study of French culture, see Theodore Zeldin, *France: 1848–1945*. 2 vols. (Oxford: Oxford University Press, 1973).

7. The music was not, however, a result of any Poulenc–de Brunhoff friendship. See Patrick O'Connor, "Babar's Birthday Treats," *Times Literary Supplement*, 26 June 1981, 726, for the genesis of the work. *The Story of Babar the Little Elephant* debuted in England in 1949, with Poulenc himself accompanying Noël Coward; many illustrious pairs have performed it since.

8. Justin Wintle and Emma Fisher, *The Pied Pipers* (New York: Paddington Press, 1974), 85, 86.

9. For interesting, though sometimes reductionist, sociopolitical analyses of Babar's world see Ariel Dorfman, *The Empire's Old Clothes* (New York: Pantheon, 1983), 17–64 (hereafter cited in text); Harry C. Payne, "The Reign of King Babar," *Children's Literature* 11 (1983): 96–108; Patrick Richardson, "Teach your Baby to Rule," in *Suitable for Children? Controversies in Children's Literature* (Berkeley: University of California Press, 1976), 179–83 (hereafter cited in text).

10. Peter Vaughan, "At 50, Babar's No White Elephant," *The Minneapolis Star*, 20 November 1981, 3A, B.
11. Loyd Grossman, "Babar the Architect," *Harpers & Queen*, May 1984, 86–88.
12. *"Picnic at Babar's," Junior Bookshelf* 14, no. 5 (November 1950): 194–95; Karl Miller, "Welfare King," *New Statesman*, 9 November 1962; Margery Fisher, "Babar's Mystery," *Growing Point* 18, no. 2 (July 1979): 3552.

Chapter Two

1. Jean de Brunhoff, *The Story of Babar the Little Elephant*, trans. Merle S. Haas (New York: Harrison Smith and Robert Haas, 1933) 3; hereafter cited as *Story*. A note by A. A. Milne introduced Methuen's edition of *The Story of Babar*, 1934, and was reprinted on the back dustjacket of Random House's 1984 facsimile volume.

2. Margaret Wise Brown, *The Dead Bird*, illus. Remy Charlip (New York: Young Scott Books, 1938); there is no evidence, however, that Brown was influenced by *The Story of Babar*.

3. Eleanor Graham, "The Genius of de Brunhoff: the Creator of the Babar Books," *Junior Bookshelf* 5, no. 2 (January 1941): 49–55.

4. André Francois's *Les larmes de crocodile* (*Crocodile Tears*) (Paris: Robert Delpire, 1967) has an almost identical scene in which a champagne-drinking croc lounges against a mantel, telling "les jolies histoires" to adoring, fez-clad listeners. Francois even puts his hero in a bathtub and populates the book with later Babarian types—dromedaries, pelicans, and "beaux oiseaux," surely a nod to his countryman's work.

5. Ann M. Hildebrand, "Jean de Brunhoff's Advice to Youth: The *Babar* Books as Books of Courtesy," *Children's Literature* 11 (1983): 76–96.

6. E. H. Gombrich, *Art and Illusion* (Princeton, N.J.: Princeton University Press, 1960), 334.

7. For the family habits of African elephants see Cynthia Moss, *Elephant Memories: Thirteen Years in the Life of an Elephant Family* (New York: William Morrow, 1988), and Sallie Tisdale, "The Only Harmless Great Thing," *New Yorker*, 23 January 1989, 38–88.

8. Jean's first drawings called Cécile's invention only "Bébé." Whether he finally chose "Babar" for its sound or to stir memories of the sixteenth-century Indian ruler Babur or Babar even Laurent does not know.

9. Jean de Brunhoff, *The Travels of Babar*, trans. Merle S. Haas (New York: Harrison Smith and Robert Haas, 1934; hereafter cited as *Travels*.

10. Josephine Baker's black stereotype and its impact on Paris is chronicled in Lynn Haney, *Naked at the Feast: A Biography of Josephine Baker* (New York: Dodd, Mead, 1981), 49ff. See also Phyllis Rose, *Jazz Cleopatra: Josephine Baker in Her Time* (New York: Doubleday, 1989).

11. Jean de Brunhoff, *Babar the King,* trans. Merle S. Haas (New York: Harrison Smith and Robert Haas, 1935 3; hereafter cited as *King.*

12. For the reality behind the elephant Versailles see *Versailles: A Garden in Four Seasons,* photographs by Jacques Dubois (New York: Vendome Press, 1983).

13. See August A. Imholtz, Jr., "Sanskrit verses in a Babar book," *Children's Literature in Education* 12 (1981): 207–8, for an informed, probably tongue-in-cheek, reading of the mammoth's song. Jean did not, however, know Sanskrit.

14. Edmund Leach, "Babar's Civilization Analyzed," *New Society,* 20 December 1962, 16.

Chapter Three

1. Jean de Brunhoff, *A.B.C. of Babar,* trans. Merle S. Haas (New York: Random House, 1936); hereafter cited as *A.B.C.*

2. Jean de Brunhoff, *Zephir's Holidays,* trans. Merle S. Haas (New York: Random House, 1937) 3, see p. 78; hereafter cited as *Zephir.* Subsequent American editions were titled *Babar and Zephir* to identify the book more clearly.

3. Bettina Hurlimann, "Jean de Brunhoff and the Benevolent Monarchy of King Babar," in *Three Centuries of Children's Books in Europe* (Cleveland and New York: World Publishing Co., 1968), 195–200. Unfortunately, because Hurlimann was one of the few early sources of de Brunhoff biography, her misinformation affected nearly all Babar scholarship before the mid-1980s, my own included.

4. Jean de Brunhoff, *Babar and His Children,* trans. Merle S. Haas (New York: Random House, 1938), 3; hereafter cited as *Children.* The first American edition was unpaged; curiously, the 1989 "facsimile" had numbered pages. Methuen's edition (1938) retained the original *Daily Sketch* title of *Babar at Home.*

5. Jean de Brunhoff, *Babar and Father Christmas,* trans. Merle S. Haas (New York: Random House, 1940), 7; hereafter cited as *Father Christmas.* The original American first edition was unpaged; here, too, the "facsimile" edition (1987) had *numbered* pages.

6. See Francis P. Church, "Yes, Virginia, there is a Santa Claus," *New York Sun,* 21 September 1897.

7. Enid Blyton, *The Babar Story Book,* illus. F. Openshaw (London: Methuen, 1941). This odd little (5-by-7-inch) wartime edition was printed

also in Australia by Pikven & Stevens in 1943. Laurent de Brunhoff, *Les aventures de Babar* (Paris: Hachette, 1959).

Chapter Four

1. Laurent de Brunhoff, *Babar's Cousin: That Rascal Arthur,* trans. Merle S. Haas (New York: Random House, 1948), 3; hereafter cited as *Arthur.*
2. Laurent de Brunhoff, *Babar's Picnic,* trans. Merle S. Haas (New York: Random House, 1949), 3; hereafter cited as *Picnic.*
3. "Babar Pays Us a Visit at Last," *Life,* 26 November 1965.
4. Laurent de Brunhoff, *Babar's Visit to Bird Island* (New York: Random House, 1952), 4, 5; hereafter cited as *Bird Island.*
5. Laurent de Brunhoff, *Babar's Fair,* trans. Merle S. Haas (New York: Random House, 1955), 8; hereafter cited as *Fair.*
6. Laurent de Brunhoff, *Babar and the Professor,* trans. Merle S. Haas (New York: Random House, 1957), n.p.; hereafter cited as *Professor.*
7. Laurent de Brunhoff, *A tue-tête,* text by Jacques Lanzman (Paris: Juilliard, 1957).
8. Laurent de Brunhoff, *Babar's Castle,* trans. Merle S. Haas (New York: Random House, 1962), 5; hereafter cited as *Castle.*

Chapter Five

1. Laurent de Brunhoff, *Serafina the Giraffe* (Cleveland: World Publishing Co., 1961); *Serafina's Lucky Find* (Cleveland: World Publishing Co., 1962); *Captain Serafina* (Cleveland: World Publishing Co., 1963); hereafter cited as *Serafina, Lucky Find,* and *Captain,* respectively.
2. Laurent de Brunhoff, *Anatole and His Donkey,* trans. Richard Howard (New York: Macmillan, 1963), n.p.; hereafter cited as *Anatole.*
3. Laurent de Brunhoff, *Babar's French Lessons* (New York: Random House, 1963); *Babar's Spanish Lessons,* Spanish words by Roberto Eyzaguirre (New York: Random House, 1965); hereafter cited as *Lessons.*
4. Laurent de Brunhoff, *Bonhomme,* trans. Richard Howard (New York: Pantheon, 1965); hereafter cited as *Bonhomme 1.*
5. Tomi Ungerer, *Moon Man* (New York: Harper & Row, 1967).
6. Laurent de Brunhoff, *Babar Comes to America,* trans. M. Jean Craig (New York: Random House, 1965); hereafter cited as *America.* Hachette published the adventure in two parts, *Babar à New York* in 1965 and *Babar en Amérique* in 1967.
7. Robert Phelps, "Travel Stickers on His Trunk," *New York Herald Tribune Book Week,* 31 October 1965, 2.

8. Alison Lurie, "Babar Comes to America," *New York Review of Books*, 9 December 1965, 38.

9. Laurent de Brunhoff, *Babar Loses His Crown* (New York: Random House, 1967), 8; hereafter cited as *Crown*.

10. Laurent de Brunhoff, *Babar's Games* (New York: Random House, 1968); hereafter cited as *Games*. *Babar's Moon Trip* (New York: Random House, 1969); hereafter cited as *Moon Trip*.

11. Laurent de Brunhoff, *Babar's Trunk*, trans. Merle S. Haas (New York: Random House, 1969); hereafter cited as *Trunk*. *Babar's Other Trunk* (New York: Random House, 1971); hereafter cited as *Other Trunk*. *Babar's Bookmobile* (New York: Random House, 1974); hereafter cited as *Bookmobile*.

12. Laurent de Brunhoff, *Babar's Birthday Surprise* (New York: Random House, 1970); hereafter cited as *Surprise*.

13. Laurent de Brunhoff, *Gregory and the Lady Turtle in the Valley of Music Trees*, trans. Richard Howard (New York: Pantheon, 1971); hereafter cited as *Gregory*.

Chapter Six

1. Laurent de Brunhoff, *Babar Visits Another Planet*, trans. Merle S. Haas (New York: Random House, 1972); hereafter cited as *Planet*.

2. See especially Karla Kuskin, "*Babar Visits Another Planet*," *Saturday Review of Education*, 10 March 1973, 67–68.

3. William Pene du Bois, *The Twenty-one Balloons* (New York: Lothrop, 1948).

4. Laurent de Brunhoff, *Meet Babar and His Family* (New York: Random House, 1973); hereafter cited as *Family*. *Babar Saves the Day* (New York: Random House, 1976); hereafter cited as *Saves the Day*. *Babar Learns to Cook* (New York: Random House, 1978); hereafter cited as *Learns to Cook*. *Babar the Magician* (New York: Random House, 1980); hereafter cited as *Magician*.

5. Laurent de Brunhoff, *Bonhomme and the Huge Beast*, trans. Richard Howard (New York: Pantheon, 1974); hereafter cited as *Bonhomme 2*.

6. Laurent de Brunhoff, *Babar and the Wully-Wully* (New York: Random House, 1975); hereafter cited as *Wully*.

7. Laurent de Brunhoff, *Babar's Mystery* (New York: Random House, 1978); hereafter cited as *Mystery*.

8. See Auro Roselli, *Cats of the Eiffel Tower*, illus. L. de Brunhoff (New York: Dial, 1967), for expressive sepia-and-black line renderings of the animal that Laurent considered "too hard to draw."

9. Laurent de Brunhoff, *The One Pig with Horns*, trans. Richard Howard (New York: Pantheon, 1979); hereafter cited as *Pig*.

10. See Claire Wilson, "De Brunhoff, Babar, and one pig with horns," *American Bookseller*, March 1979; Harold C. K. Rice, *"The One Pig With Horns," New York Time Book Review*, 29 April 1979, 29; Barbara S. Worth, *"The One Pig with Horns," Children's Book Review Service*, June 1979, 101.

11. Laurent de Brunhoff, *Babar's Little Library* (New York: Random House, 1980); hereafter cited as *Little Library*.

12. Laurent de Brunhoff, *Babar and the Ghost* (New York: Random House, 1981); hereafter cited as *Ghost 1*. *Babar the Ghost: An Easy-to-Read Version* (New York: Random House, 1986); hereafter cited as *Ghost 2*.

13. Jean and Laurent de Brunhoff, *Babar's Anniversary Album: 6 Favorite Stories by Jean and Laurent de Brunhoff*, with an introduction by Maurice Sendak (New York: Random House, 1981); hereafter cited as *Album*.

14. *Fifty Years of Babar* (New York: International Exhibitions Foundation, 1983). See also Frank J. Prial, "A Party for Babar, The Elephant King," New York *Times,* 2 August, 1981.

15. Laurent de Brunhoff, *Babar's A.B.C.* (New York: Random House, 1983); hereafter cited as *Babar's A.B.C. Babar's Book of Color* (New York: Random House, 1984); hereafter cited as *Color. Babar's Counting Book* (New York: Random House, 1986); hereafter cited as *Counting.*

16. Laurent de Brunhoff, *Babar's Little Girl* (New York: Random House, 1987); hereafter cited as *Little Girl.*

17. Laurent de Brunhoff, "Christmas with Babar and Baby Isabelle," *Woman's Day,* 22 December 1987, 61–64; hereafter cited as "Christmas." *Babar's Little Circus Star* (New York: Random House, 1988); hereafter cited as *Star. Babar's Busy Year* (New York: Random House, 1989); hereafter cited as *Busy Year. A Babar Book: Isabelle's New Friend* (New York: Random House, 1990); hereafter cited as *Friend.*

18. Laurent de Brunhoff, *Babar's Adventures, 1988 Calendar; Babar's Adventures, 1989 Calendar; Babar in Hollywood, 1990 Calendar; Babar in History, 1991 Calendar* (New York: Stewart, Tabori & Chang, 1987, 1988, 1989, 1990).

Chapter Seven

1. Arthur Yorinks, *Hey, Al,* illus. Richard Egielski (New York: Farrar, Straus & Giroux, 1986); Russell Hoban, *Bedtime for Frances,* illus. Lillian Hoban (New York: Harper & Row, 1960); James Marshall, *George and Martha* (Boston: Houghton Mifflin, 1972); Else Holmelund Minarik,

Little Bear, illus. Maurice Sendak (New York: Harper, 1957); Arnold Lobel, *Frog and Toad Are Friends* (New York: Harper & Row, 1970).

2. Marguerite MacKellar Mitchell, "Histoire de Babar/Le Voyage de Babar by Jean de Brunhoff," *Horn Book* 9 (1933): 29, 30.

3. C. S. Lewis, "On Three Ways of Writing for Children," *Horn Book* 39 (1963): 469.

4. Arthur Applebee, *The Child's Concept of Story* (Chicago: University of Chicago Press, 1989), 30–53.

Selected Bibliography

Primary Works

Jean de Brunhoff

A.B.C. of Babar. New York: Random House, 1936.
Babar and Father Christmas. New York: Random House, 1940.
Babar and His Children. New York: Random House, 1938.
Babar the King. New York: Harrison Smith and Robert Haas, 1935.
Babar's Anniversary Album. New York: Random House, 1981.
The Story of Babar the Little Elephant. New York: Harrison Smith and Robert Haas, 1933.
The Travels of Babar. New York: Harrison Smith and Robert Haas, 1934.
Zephir's Holidays. New York: Random House, 1937.

Laurent de Brunhoff

Anatole and His Donkey. New York: Macmillan, 1963.
A tue-tête. Paris: Juillard, 1957.
Babar Comes to America. New York: Random House, 1965.
Babar and the Ghost. New York: Random House, 1981.
Babar and the Ghost. Easy to Read Edition. New York: Random House, 1986.
Babar in History, Calendar for 1991. New York: Stewart, Tabori, & Chang, 1990.
Babar in Hollywood, Calendar for 1990. New York: Stewart, Tabori & Chang, 1989.
Babar Learns to Cook. New York: Random House, 1978.
Babar Loses His Crown. New York: Random House, 1967.
Babar the Magician. New York: Random House, 1980.
Babar and the Professor. New York: Random House, 1957.
Babar Saves the Day. New York: Random House, 1976.
Babar Visits Another Planet. New York: Random House, 1972.

Selected Bibliography

Babar and the Wully-Wully. New York: Random House, 1975.
Babar's A.B.C. New York: Random House, 1983.
Babar's Adventures, Calendar for 1988. New York: Stewart, Tabori & Chang, 1987.
Babar's Adventures, Calendar for 1989. New York: Stewart, Tabori & Chang, 1988.
Babar's Anniversary Album. New York: Random House, 1981.
Babar's Birthday Surprise. New York: Random House, 1970.
Babar's Book of Color. New York: Random House, 1984.
Babar's Bookmobile. New York: Random House, 1974.
Babar's Busy Year. New York: Random House, 1989.
Babar's Castle. New York: Random House, 1962.
Babar's Counting Book. New York: Random House, 1986.
Babar's Cousin: That Rascal Arthur. New York: Random House, 1948.
Babar's Fair. New York: Random House, 1955.
Babar's French Lessons. New York: Random House, 1963.
Babar's Games. New York: Random House, 1968.
Babar's Little Circus Star. New York: Random House, 1988.
Babar's Little Girl. New York: Random House, 1987.
Babar's Little Library. New York: Random House, 1980.
Babar's Moon Trip. New York: Random House, 1969.
Babar's Mystery. New York: Random House, 1978.
Babar's Other Trunk. New York: Random House, 1971.
Babar's Picnic. New York: Random House, 1949.
Babar's Spanish Lessons. New York: Random House, 1965.
Babar's Trunk. New York: Random House, 1969.
Babar's Visit to Bird Island. New York: Random House, 1952.
Bonhomme. New York: Pantheon, 1965.
Bonhomme and the Huge Beast. New York: Pantheon, 1974.
Captain Serafina. Cleveland: World Publishing Co., 1963.
"Christmas with Babar & Baby Isabelle." *Woman's Day,* 22 December, 1987.
Gregory and the Lady Turtle in the Valley of the Music Trees. New York: Pantheon, 1971.
Isabelle's New Friend. New York: Random House, 1990.
Meet Babar and His Family. New York: Random House, 1973.
The One Pig with Horns. New York: Pantheon, 1979.
Serafina the Giraffe. Cleveland: World Publishing Co., 1961.
Serafina's Lucky Find. Cleveland: World Publishing Co., 1962.

Secondary Works

Books and Parts of Books

The Art of Babar: Drawings and Watercolors by Jean and Laurent de Brunhoff. Alexandria, Virginia: Art Services International, 1989. Paperback catalogue and overview of the 1990–91 touring exhibit of de Brunhoff paintings, with a preface by Laurent de Brunhoff and small sampling of pictures.

Dorfman, Ariel. "Of Elephants and Ducks." In *The Empire's Old Clothes: What the Lone Ranger, Babar, and Other Innocent Heroes Do To Our Minds,* 17–64. New York Pantheon, 1983. Without humor, points out the essentially colonialist thinking behind Babar's (and Disney's) perspective in which "primitive" cultures must be dominated by and assimilated into advanced ones.

Fifty Years of Babar: Watercolors by Jean and Laurent de Brunhoff. New York: International Exhibitions Foundation, 1983. Paperback catalog of the 1983–84 touring exhibit of de Brunhoff paintings with photographs, reproductions, a preface and catalog by Laurent de Brunhoff, Maurice Sendak's introduction to *Anniversary Album,* and short biographical sketches.

Hildebrand, Ann M. "Jean de Brunhoff." In *Writers for Children,* edited by Jane Bingham, 91–96. New York: Scribner's, 1987. A critical biographical study of the first seven Babar books.

Hurlimann, Bettina. "Jean de Brunhoff and the benevolent monarchy of King Babar." In *Three Centuries of Children's Books in Europe,* 195–200. Cleveland and New York: World Publishing Co., 1968. Published first in Europe, and translated and edited by Brian Alderson, the major source in translation of biography and criticism of de Brunhoffs up to this time.

Richardson, Patrick. "Teach your Baby to Rule." In *Suitable for Children?: Controversies in Children's Literature,* edited by Nicholas Tucker, 179–83. Berkeley: University of California Press, 1976. Reprinted from *New Society,* a half-serious Marxist reading of Jean's books showing Babar as a fascist-militarist dictator who has gained power by coups d'état and manipulation of the masses.

Sale, Roger. "Introduction: Child Reading and Man Reading." In *Fairy Tales and After: From Snow White to E. B. White,* 1–22. Cambridge: Harvard Univ. Press, 1978. A reflection on mainly Jean's works that emphasizes the Babars' reassuring impassivity in the face of life's ups and downs.

Sendak, Maurice. "Homage to Babar on His 50th Birthday." In *Babar's Anniversary Album: 6 Favorite Stories by Jean and Laurent de*

Brunhoff, 7–15. New York: Random House, 1981. An overview of de Brunhoff biographies and themes, mainly Jean's, with attention to the art of illustration and extended photograph captions by Laurent.

Weber, Nicholas Fox. *The Art of Babar.* New York: Abrams, 1989. Many reproductions of original art, extensive biographical detail about both de Brunhoffs, and some enthusiastic art criticism. For the first time, Laurent's work is discussed on its own.

Wintle, Justin, and Emma Fisher. "Laurent de Brunhoff." In *The Pied Pipers,* 78–98. New York: Paddington Press, 1974. An interview in which Fisher discusses both men's work with Laurent.

Articles

Graham, Eleanor. "The Genius of de Brunhoff: The Creator of the Babar Books." *Junior Bookshelf* (January 1941): 49–55. A critical overview of Jean de Brunhoff's contribution to children's literature and how benevolence, child-centeredness, and nursery morality inform the Babars.

Grossman, Loyd. "Babar the Architect." *Harpers & Queen,* May 1984, 86–88. Slightly tongue in cheek, parallels urban development in Célesteville with real architectural styles from Roman times.

Hildebrand, Ann M. "Jean de Brunhoff's Advice to Youth: The *Babar* Books as Books of Courtesy." *Children's Literature* 11 (1983): 76–96. Traces in Jean's stories the major elements of courtesy literature from medieval times through the eighteenth century.

Imholtz, August A., Jr. "Sanskrit verses in a Babar book." *Children's Literature in Education* 12 (1981): 207–8. Discusses rather persuasively the probably nonexistent relationship between ancient Sanskrit patterns and the Babars.

Leach, Edmund. "Babar's Civilization Analyzed." *New Society,* 20 December 1962, 16–17. Half-serious, an anthropologist's hierarchy of rule that aligns white men and elephants at the top and relegates wild beasts and domestic animals to the bottom of a colonialist social scale.

Payne, Harry C. "The Reign of King Babar." *Children's Literature* 11 (1983): 96–108. One of the few who considers *A.B.C. de Babar* when putting Jean's books into political-historical-cultural perspective.

Piper, John. "Babar the Elephant." *The Spectator,* 5867 6 December 1940, 611. Perhaps the most literate and thoughtful of the relatively few obituary essays in English, placing Jean's work in the mainstream of twentieth century art.

Pissard, Annie. "Long Live Babar." *The Lion and the Unicorn* 7/8 (1983/ 4): 70–77. An 1981 anniversary overview published originally in French and translated by Jules Gelernt brings a Continental perspective to de Brunhoff art.

Wernick, Robert. "A lovable elephant that youngsters never ever forget." *Smithsonian Magazine,* July 1984), 90–96. A literate overview of both de Brunhoffs' lives and work, with reproductions; published at the end of the first American tour.

Index

The Author

Ann Meinzen Hildebrand received her Ph.D. from Kent State University, where she is a visiting associate professor of English and teaches children's literature. Her essays, on a variety of secular and religious topics in children's literature, include "Jean de Brunhoff's Advice to Youth: The *Babar* Books as Books of Courtesy" and a critical biographical study of Jean de Brunhoff. She is married to a fellow professor of English and has two grown children.

The Editor

Ruth K. MacDonald is a professor of English and head of the Department of English and Philosophy at Purdue University. She received her B.A. and M.A. in English from the University of Connecticut, her Ph.D. in English from Rutgers University, and her M.B.A. from the University of Texas at El Paso. To Twayne's United States and English Authors series she has contributed the volumes on Louisa May Alcott, Beatrix Potter, and Dr. Seuss. She is the author of *Literature for Children in England and America, 1646–1774* (1982).